First World War
and Army of Occupation
War Diary
France, Belgium and Germany

17 DIVISION
Divisional Troops
79 Brigade Royal Field Artillery
13 July 1915 - 31 March 1919

WO95/1991/4

The Naval & Military Press Ltd
www.nmarchive.com
Published in association with The National Archives

Published by

The Naval & Military Press Ltd

Unit 10 Ridgewood Industrial Park,

Uckfield, East Sussex,

TN22 5QE England

Tel: +44 (0) 1825 749494

www.naval-military-press.com

www.nmarchive.com

This diary has been reprinted in facsimile from the original. Any imperfections are inevitably reproduced and the quality may fall short of modern type and cartographic standards.

© Crown Copyright
Images reproduced by permission of The National Archives, London, England, 2015.

Contents

Document type	Place/Title	Date From	Date To
Heading	WO95/1991/4		
Heading	17th Division 19th Brigade R.F.A. July 1915-Mar 1919		
Heading	17th Division. "B"/79 Battery R.F.A. Vol. 114-30.7.15		
War Diary	Le Havre	14/07/1915	14/07/1915
War Diary	Lumbres	15/07/1915	15/07/1915
War Diary	Wismes	18/07/1915	18/07/1915
War Diary	Campagne	18/07/1915	18/07/1915
War Diary	Caestre	19/07/1915	19/07/1915
War Diary	La Clytte	26/07/1915	30/07/1915
War Diary	La Clytte	31/07/1915	31/07/1915
Heading	17th Division 79th Bde. R.F.A. Vol. I Jly & Aug No/15. Mar 19		
War Diary	Winchester Pitt Cornet Camp.	13/07/1915	13/07/1915
War Diary	Harve	14/07/1915	14/07/1915
War Diary	Wismes and. Affringues	15/07/1915	17/07/1915
War Diary	Campagne	18/07/1915	18/07/1915
War Diary	Caestre	20/07/1915	27/07/1915
War Diary	Boeschepe	27/07/1915	18/08/1915
War Diary	Dickebusch	19/08/1915	31/08/1915
Map	17th Division 79th Bde. R.F.A. Vol. II Sept 15		
War Diary	Dickebusch	01/09/1915	30/09/1915
Miscellaneous	17th Division 79th Bde. R.F.A. Vol 3. Oct 15		
War Diary	Dickebusch	01/10/1915	22/10/1915
War Diary	Kruitstraat	23/10/1915	31/10/1915
Heading	14th Division 79th Bde R.F.A. Vol 4 Nov 15		
War Diary	Kruitstraat	01/11/1915	10/11/1915
War Diary	Ypres (Dixmude Gate)	11/11/1915	30/11/1915
Heading	17th Div 79th Bde. R.F.A. Vol 5		
War Diary	Ypres (Dixmude Gate)	01/12/1915	18/12/1915
War Diary	Ypres	19/12/1915	08/01/1916
War Diary	Tournehem	08/01/1916	31/01/1916
Heading	79th Bde. R.F.A. Vol 6		
War Diary	79th Bde. R.F.A. Vol. 7		
War Diary	Tournehem	01/02/1916	06/02/1916
War Diary	Steenvoorde	06/02/1916	06/02/1916
War Diary	Dickebusch.	07/02/1916	29/02/1916
Heading	79 RFA Vol 8		
War Diary	Dickebusch	01/03/1916	13/03/1916
War Diary	Pradelles	14/03/1916	22/03/1916
War Diary	Armentiere	23/03/1916	31/03/1916
War Diary	Armentieres	01/04/1916	30/04/1916
Heading	Herewith War Diary For May 1916. of 79th Bde R.F.A.	02/06/1916	02/06/1916
War Diary	Armentieres	01/05/1916	17/05/1916
War Diary	Vieux Berquin Renescure Nielles-Lez-Blequin	18/05/1916	25/05/1916
War Diary	Nielles-Les-Blequin	26/05/1916	10/06/1916
War Diary	Therouanne	10/06/1916	10/06/1916
War Diary	Wavrans	11/06/1916	11/06/1916
War Diary	Neuvillette	12/06/1916	12/06/1916
War Diary	Talmas	13/06/1916	13/06/1916
War Diary	Heilly	14/06/1916	14/06/1916

War Diary	Ville-Sows-Corbie	15/06/1916	22/06/1916
War Diary	Becourt Becordel	23/06/1916	24/06/1916
War Diary	Becordel	24/06/1916	30/06/1916
Heading	17th Div. XV. Corps. War Diary Headquarters. 79th Brigade. R.F.A. July 1916		
War Diary	Becordel	01/07/1916	15/07/1916
War Diary	Fricourt	15/07/1916	23/07/1916
War Diary	Dernancourt	24/07/1916	31/07/1916
Miscellaneous	79th Bde R.F.A.	31/07/1916	31/07/1916
Heading	17th Divisional Artillery. 79th Brigade Royal Field Artillery. August 1916. Ammunition expenditure. Casualties. Casualties animals.		
War Diary	Dernancourt	01/08/1916	01/08/1916
War Diary	Near Bazentin-Le-Grand	02/08/1916	20/08/1916
War Diary	Bonnay	21/08/1916	22/08/1916
War Diary	Cardonnette	23/08/1916	23/08/1916
War Diary	Occoches	24/08/1916	24/08/1916
War Diary	Gaudiempre	25/08/1916	31/08/1916
Miscellaneous	79th. Bde R.F.A.	00/08/1916	00/08/1916
War Diary	Sailly-Au-Bois	01/09/1916	20/09/1916
War Diary	Pas.	21/09/1916	21/09/1916
War Diary	Bealcourt Villeroy	22/09/1916	30/09/1916
Miscellaneous	79th Bde R.F.A.	00/09/1916	00/09/1916
War Diary	Pas Huts	01/10/1916	02/10/1916
War Diary	Hebuterne	03/10/1916	05/10/1916
War Diary	Sailly Au Bois	06/10/1916	12/10/1916
War Diary	Hebuterne	13/10/1916	16/10/1916
War Diary	Pas Huts	17/10/1916	18/10/1916
War Diary	Albert	19/10/1916	31/10/1916
Miscellaneous	79th Bde. R.F.A.	00/10/1916	00/10/1916
War Diary	Albert	01/11/1916	05/11/1916
War Diary	Albert (positions at Mouquet Farm)	06/11/1916	21/11/1916
War Diary	Meaulte	22/11/1916	30/11/1916
Miscellaneous	79th Bde. R.F.A.	00/11/1916	00/11/1916
War Diary	Meaulte	01/12/1916	11/12/1916
War Diary	Ginchy. (near)	12/12/1916	28/12/1916
War Diary	Ginchy.	29/12/1916	31/12/1916
Miscellaneous	79th Brigade R.F.A.		
War Diary	Ginchy. (near)	01/01/1917	31/01/1917
Miscellaneous	79th Brigade R.F.A. War Diary For January 1917. Appendix.	00/01/1917	00/01/1917
War Diary	Ginchy (near)	01/02/1917	28/02/1917
Miscellaneous	79th Bde. R.F.A. Appendix. to War Diary for February 1917	00/02/1917	00/02/1917
War Diary	Ginchy (near)	01/03/1917	07/03/1917
War Diary	Albert Wagon Line Guns at Martinpuich	08/03/1917	15/03/1917
War Diary	Albert	16/03/1917	18/03/1917
War Diary	Puchevillers	19/03/1917	20/03/1917
War Diary	Bealcourt.	21/03/1917	24/03/1917
War Diary	St Michel.	25/03/1917	26/03/1917
War Diary	Bray.	27/03/1917	31/03/1917
Miscellaneous	Appendix to War Diary for March. 1917	02/04/1917	02/04/1917
War Diary	C Camp S.W. of Bray.	01/04/1917	08/04/1917
War Diary	St Catherine	09/04/1917	09/04/1917
War Diary	Bray. Wagon Lines	09/04/1917	09/04/1917
War Diary	Arras	10/04/1917	14/04/1917

Type	Location	From	To
War Diary	Monchy-Le-Preux	15/04/1917	19/04/1917
War Diary	Monchy.	20/04/1917	30/04/1917
Miscellaneous	Appendix. to War Diary For April 1917	00/04/1917	00/04/1917
War Diary	Monchy-Le-Preux	01/05/1917	03/05/1917
War Diary	Monchy	03/05/1917	12/05/1917
War Diary	Monchy-Le-Preux	13/05/1917	16/05/1917
War Diary	Henin-Sur-Cojeul	17/05/1917	17/05/1917
War Diary	Henin.	18/05/1917	20/05/1917
War Diary	Henin-Sur-Cojeul	20/05/1917	22/05/1917
War Diary	Arras.	23/05/1917	25/05/1917
War Diary	Monchy. (near)	26/05/1917	29/05/1917
War Diary	Monchy-Le-Preux.	30/05/1917	31/05/1917
Miscellaneous	Appendix May 1917 79th FAB		
War Diary	Monchy Le Preux	01/06/1917	13/06/1917
War Diary	Monchy.	14/06/1917	16/06/1917
War Diary	Arras	17/06/1917	17/06/1917
War Diary	Anzin	18/06/1917	18/06/1917
War Diary	Near Fampoux.	19/06/1917	30/06/1917
Miscellaneous	Appendix		
War Diary	Near Fampoux. (on the Scarpe)	01/07/1917	03/07/1917
War Diary	Near Fampoux	03/07/1917	13/07/1917
War Diary	Fampoux	13/07/1917	14/07/1917
War Diary	Near Fampoux.	15/07/1917	31/07/1917
Miscellaneous	Appendix		
War Diary	Near. Fampoux.	01/08/1917	31/08/1917
Miscellaneous	Appendix	00/08/1917	00/08/1917
War Diary	Near Fampoux	01/09/1917	24/09/1917
War Diary	Fampoux	25/09/1917	27/09/1917
War Diary	Anzin St Aubin	28/09/1917	30/09/1917
Miscellaneous	Appendix	00/09/1917	00/09/1917
Diagram etc	Raid on Crust Trench 9 pm 16th Sept/17 by 10th Sherwoods & 8. RE.		
Diagram etc	Raid on Wit Trench 16th-17 Sept. 1917		
Diagram etc	Wit Trench Raid.		
War Diary	Anzin-St. Aubin.	01/10/1917	01/10/1917
War Diary	Nr. Arras.	02/10/1917	03/10/1917
War Diary	Near Proven	04/10/1917	05/10/1917
War Diary	Elverdinghe	06/10/1917	09/10/1917
War Diary	Near Langemarck	10/10/1917	25/10/1917
War Diary	Poelcappelle	26/10/1917	31/10/1917
Miscellaneous	Appendix	00/10/1917	00/10/1917
War Diary	Schreiboom Near Poelcappelle	01/11/1917	11/11/1917
War Diary	Ochtezeele	12/11/1917	30/11/1917
Miscellaneous	Appendix.	01/12/1917	01/12/1917
War Diary	Ochtezeele	01/12/1917	16/12/1917
War Diary	Crecques	17/12/1917	17/12/1917
War Diary	Tangry.	18/12/1917	20/12/1917
War Diary	Rebreuviette	21/12/1917	21/12/1917
War Diary	Fosseux	22/12/1917	26/12/1917
War Diary	Havrincourt wagon lines at Beaulencourt	26/12/1917	28/12/1917
War Diary	Havrincourt	29/12/1917	31/12/1917
Miscellaneous	Appendix	01/01/1917	01/01/1917
War Diary	Havrincourt	01/01/1918	03/01/1918
War Diary	Hermies.	04/01/1918	31/01/1918
Miscellaneous	Appendix	01/02/1918	01/02/1918
War Diary	Hermies	01/02/1918	28/02/1918

Miscellaneous	Appendix	28/02/1918	28/02/1918
Heading	17th Div. Headquarters 79th Brigade. R.F.A. March 1918		
War Diary	Hermies.	01/03/1918	23/03/1918
War Diary	Villers-Au-Bois	23/03/1918	24/03/1918
War Diary	Ligny-Tilloy.	24/03/1918	24/03/1918
War Diary	Pozieres	25/03/1918	25/03/1918
War Diary	La Boisselle	25/03/1918	25/03/1918
War Diary	Albert	25/03/1918	26/03/1918
War Diary	Bouzincourt.	27/03/1918	28/03/1918
Miscellaneous	All Batteries in Action at Senlis, Covering 50th Inf Bde.	02/04/1918	02/04/1918
Miscellaneous	79th Bde RFA-War Diary-March Appendix.	02/04/1918	02/04/1918
Miscellaneous	A few notes by Major C.H.A Huxtable on Operations of 79th Brigade R.F.A. (17th Division) V Corps, 21st-23rd March 1918	21/03/1918	21/03/1918
Miscellaneous	A few notes by Major C.H.A Huxtable DSO. MC. on the operations of the 79th Brigade R.F.A. (17th Division) V. Corps front. 21st-23rd March 1918	21/03/1918	21/03/1918
Heading	17th Divisional Artillery War Diary 79th Brigade R.F.A. April 1918 Appendix-See last page		
War Diary	Senlis	01/04/1918	12/04/1918
War Diary	Toutencourt Area.	13/04/1918	21/04/1918
War Diary	Englebelmer.	22/04/1918	30/04/1918
Miscellaneous	Appendix.	30/04/1918	30/04/1918
War Diary	Englebelmer	01/05/1918	04/05/1918
War Diary	Mesnil	05/05/1918	26/05/1918
War Diary	Beaussart	27/05/1918	28/05/1918
War Diary	Mailly-Maillet	29/05/1918	31/05/1918
Miscellaneous	Appendix.	00/05/1918	00/05/1918
War Diary	Mailly-Maillet.	01/06/1918	24/06/1918
War Diary	Toutencourt	25/06/1918	25/06/1918
War Diary	Lealvillers	26/06/1918	30/06/1918
Miscellaneous	Appendix	30/06/1918	30/06/1918
War Diary	Bussy-Les-Daours	01/07/1918	01/07/1918
War Diary	Hamelet.	02/07/1918	04/07/1918
War Diary	Hamelet Daours	05/07/1918	06/07/1918
War Diary	Lealvillers	07/07/1918	12/07/1918
War Diary	Martinsart	13/07/1918	31/07/1918
Miscellaneous	Appendix	01/08/1918	01/08/1918
Heading	17th Divl. Artillery 79th Brigade. Royal Field Artillery. August 1918		
War Diary	Martinsart	01/08/1918	06/08/1918
War Diary	Toutencourt	07/08/1918	08/08/1918
War Diary	Blangy Tronville.	09/08/1918	10/08/1918
War Diary	Corbie	10/08/1918	11/08/1918
War Diary	Proyart	12/08/1918	16/08/1918
War Diary	Bussy-Les-Daours	17/08/1918	18/08/1918
War Diary	Toutencourt	19/08/1918	19/08/1918
War Diary	Mesnil	20/08/1918	23/08/1918
War Diary	Thiepval	24/08/1918	24/08/1918
War Diary	Courcellette	25/08/1918	25/08/1918
War Diary	Martinpuich	26/08/1918	28/08/1918
War Diary	Flers	29/08/1918	31/08/1918
Miscellaneous	79 Bde R F A	04/09/1918	04/09/1918
War Diary	Flers	01/09/1918	02/09/1918
War Diary	Bus	03/09/1918	05/09/1918

Type	Location	Start	End
War Diary	Lechelle.	06/09/1918	06/09/1918
War Diary	Fins	07/09/1918	28/09/1918
War Diary	Gouzeaucourt Wood	29/09/1918	29/09/1918
War Diary	Villers-Guislaine	30/09/1918	05/10/1918
War Diary	Honnecourt	06/10/1918	07/10/1918
War Diary	Malassise Copse	08/10/1918	08/10/1918
War Diary	Caullery.	09/10/1918	09/10/1918
War Diary	Inchy	10/10/1918	20/10/1918
War Diary	Neuvilly	21/10/1918	23/10/1918
War Diary	Vendegies-Au-Bois	24/10/1918	26/10/1918
War Diary	Clary	27/10/1918	30/10/1918
War Diary	Vendegies-Au-Bois	31/10/1918	31/10/1918
Miscellaneous	79th Bde RFA	01/10/1918	01/10/1918
War Diary	Vendegie-Au-Bois	01/11/1918	02/11/1918
War Diary	Poix-Du-Nord	03/11/1918	04/11/1918
War Diary	Futoy	04/11/1918	04/11/1918
War Diary	Tete Noir	05/11/1918	06/11/1918
War Diary	Bachant	07/11/1918	08/11/1918
War Diary	Limont-Fontaine	09/11/1918	12/11/1918
War Diary	Engle Fontaine	13/11/1918	13/11/1918
War Diary	Clary	14/11/1918	14/11/1918
War Diary	Esnes	15/11/1918	30/11/1918
Miscellaneous	79th Bde. RFA. November 1918 War Diary Appendix	01/12/1918	01/12/1918
War Diary	Esnes	01/12/1918	06/12/1918
War Diary	Manancourt	07/12/1918	07/12/1918
War Diary	Meaulte	08/12/1918	08/12/1918
War Diary	Pont Noyelles	09/12/1918	09/12/1918
War Diary	Airaines	10/12/1918	31/12/1918
Miscellaneous	Casualties	02/01/1919	02/01/1919
War Diary	Airaines	01/01/1919	31/03/1919

WO95/1991 (4)

17TH DIVISION

79TH BRIGADE R.F.A.
1915 - MAR 1919
JULY

14th Division.

"B"/79 Battery R.F.A.

Vol: I

14 - 30. 7. 15

181/6242

AE
256

Army Form C. 2118

WAR DIARY
or
INTELLIGENCE SUMMARY
(Erase heading not required.)

13/79 Batt RFA

Instructions regarding War Diaries and Intelligence Summaries are contained in F.S. Regs., Part II. and the Staff Manual respectively. Title Pages will be prepared in manuscript.

Place	Date	Hour	Summary of Events and Information	Remarks and references to Appendices
LE HAVRE	14.7.15	9 a.m.	Disembarked	
	14.7.15	9 p.m.	Entrained	
LUMBRES	15.7.15	5 p.m.	Detrained	
WISMES	18.7.15	7 p.m.	In bivouacs	
CAMPAGNE	19.7.15	9 a.m.	In bivouacs	
CAESTRE	19.7.15	8 p.m.	In bivouacs	
LACLYTTE	26.7.15	11 p.m.	In bivouacs	

Army Form C. 2118

WAR DIARY
or
INTELLIGENCE SUMMARY
(Erase heading not required.)

Instructions regarding War Diaries and Intelligence Summaries are contained in F. S. Regs., Part II. and the Staff Manual respectively. Title Pages will be prepared in manuscript.

Place	Date	Hour	Summary of Events and Information	Remarks and references to Appendices
LA CLYTTE	27.7.16	8 p.m.	Battery took up position in neighbourhood of MOUNT KEMMEL	

WAR DIARY
or
INTELLIGENCE SUMMARY

(Erase heading not required.)

Army Form C. 2118

Instructions regarding War Diaries and Intelligence Summaries are contained in F.S. Regs., Part II. and the Staff Manual respectively. Title Pages will be prepared in manuscript.

Place	Date	Hour	Summary of Events and Information	Remarks and references to Appendices
A CLYTTE 28.7.15		6 p.m.	Registered zero lines of area to be covered. Voucher references to Lucerne & inspecting Telephone lines & testing circuits	

J. Clapp Major

Place	Date	Hour	Summary of Events and Information	Remarks and references to Appendices
CUINCHY	30-7-15	11.15 a.m.	Fired three rounds for Registration purposes on the Rue chalkon J. George Lt Col mng RFA	

Army Form C. 2118

WAR DIARY
or
INTELLIGENCE SUMMARY
(Erase heading not required.)

Instructions regarding War Diaries and Intelligence Summaries are contained in F. S. Regs., Part II. and the Staff Manual respectively. Title Pages will be prepared in manuscript.

Place	Date	Hour	Summary of Events and Information	Remarks and references to Appendices
BLA CLYTTE	31-7-15	-12.0 noon	Continued digging + improving gun positions. No rounds fired.	

J.J. Keen? Lieut Major? comdg?

17th Division

121/6754

19th Bde: R.F.A.
Vol: I
July & August/15.
mss 19

Page 1

Army Form C. 2118

WAR DIARY
or
INTELLIGENCE SUMMARY

79 Bde R.F.A.

(Erase heading not required.)

Instructions regarding War Diaries and Intelligence Summaries are contained in F. S. Regs., Part II and the Staff Manual respectively. Title Pages will be prepared in manuscript.

Place	Date	Hour	Summary of Events and Information	Remarks and references to Appendices
Winchester Rifle Corner Camp.	13/7/15	5.15 a.m.	Bde left by march route. Southampton. Embarked on S.S. I.W. MILLER and other vessels. Sailed at 5 p.m. under Torpedo boat escort.	
HARUE	14/7/15	9 p.m.	Disembarked. Entrained GARE DES MERCHANDISE. en route to WISMES. Billets	
WISMES and	15/7/15 16/7/15	12 noon	Sudden order march route to CAMPAGNE. ST OMER area, where 17th Division	
AFFRINGUES	17/7/15			
CAMPAGNE	18/7/15	6 p.m.	Arrived CAESTRE. 19/7/15 6/10. HALT. refitting.	
CAESTRE	20/7/15	12 noon	Refit. Capt. MARSHALL adj. miss Lt MORGAN posted to 90th Bde RFA	
			Major WARREN joined 79th Bde and Capt HOTCHKISS posted to D.A.C.	
			Capt GILLUM posted 79th " " to 81st Bde R.F.A.	
CAESTRE	21/7/15	9.0 a.m.	Resting. " " " MAJOR SHERER " to 81st BDE R.F.A.	
	25/7/15 26/7/15	9.0 a.m. 8.0 p.m.	Resting. B/79 (Major St GEORGE KIRKE) left for LA CLYTTE to relieve battery in action of 3rd BDE REA	
	27/7/15	4.0 p.m.	Rest of Bde left for LA CLYTTE and stayed there.	
BOESCHEPE	3/8/15	8.0 p.m.	Remainder of Bde left for billets near BOESCHEPE via METERIN - BAILLEUL - BOESCHEPE Arrived about 11.30 pm	
	4/8/15	9.0 a.m.	Col ANDERSON joined up with the Brigade again.	
	4/8/15		Bde in Reserve.	
	18/8/15	" "	" " "	
DICKEBUSCH	19/8/15	9.0 p.m.	B/79 and 1 section of A&D moved into position vacated by 42nd FAB	
	20/8/15	9.0 p.m.	remaining section of A.C.D. and HQr moved into position. 74th Brindly took on from No 42 FAB	
	21/8/15	9.0 a.m.	79th Bde FAB formed part of LEFT GROUP (Col ANDERSON Commanding) other units included in the group are D/81 the Commander by CAPTAIN BRIND & BELGIAN BATTERY (CAPT de WIART)	

Pg 2

79 BDE RFA Army Form C.2118

WAR DIARY
or
INTELLIGENCE SUMMARY
(Erase heading not required.)

Place	Date	Hour	Summary of Events and Information	Remarks and references to Appendices
DICKEBUSCH	21/8/15	9.0 am	2nd & R/F section 5th Mountain Battery under 2nd Lieut. S PARLING. Position of Batteries as follows. Reference Map VOORMEZEELE 1/40,000	
			A/79 H 34 c 52 O.P. H 35 d 11	
			B/79 H 34 c 69 O.P. H 35 d 02 Single gun at I 33 a BC Single gun at O 10 37	
			C/79 H 29 d 30 O.P. I 31 a 05	
			D/79 I 26 central O.P. I 26 d 96 Headquarters Brewery H 29 c 27	Cen
			D/81 H 35 a 88 O.P. I 31 a 05	
			2 Belgian Battery H 29 c 97 O.P. I 32 a 27	
			R/5 Mountain Battery I 31 b 26 O.P. I 31 b 26	
	21/8/15 to 31/8/15		2nd & Brigade continued from PICCADILLY FARM (O 5 B 28) to O 3 a 50. This period was spent in registering zones on normal trench warfare. No incident of any note occurred during this January	Cen.

D/
699v

17th Division

79th Bde. R.F.A.
Vol: II
Sept. 15

Page 3
Army Form C. 2118

WAR DIARY
or
INTELLIGENCE SUMMARY

19th Bde R.F.A.

(Erase heading not required.)

Instructions regarding War Diaries and Intelligence Summaries are contained in F. S. Regs, Part II. and the Staff Manual respectively. Title Pages will be prepared in manuscript.

Place	Date	Hour	Summary of Events and Information	Remarks and references to Appendices
DICKEBUSCH	19/9/15 to 21/9/15		Normal Trench Warfare. No incident of any note to report. VULNERABLE GUN (01227) moved to position (H26b97)	Cen
"	22/9/15	4.0pm 5.0pm	The LEFT GROUP (including 79 F.Arty) took part in bombardment of hostile trenches between 4.0pm and 5.0pm. H.E. was used on this occasion	Cen Cen
"	24/9/15	4.0pm 5.0pm	ditto	
"	25/9/15	4 to 5.0pm 5.56 to 6.0pm	H.E. was used on this occasion. Opening of attack at HOOGE. (Ranges were fired in a demonstration against hostile trenches between MOUND (O2d12) and CAVAN (O4a75)	Cen
"	26/9/15 to 30/9/15		Normal Trench Warfare with occasional use for retaliation of hostile bombardment on firing on hostile batteries	Cen
"	30/9/15	6.30pm 9.0pm	Enemy bombardment of trenches from U29 to trench H26b60. The bombardment just couple left and of Zone of LEFT GROUP	Cen

Commanding (?) RGA
(Signed)
19th Brigade

(3)

13/7593

17th Division

79 R Bde. R.F.A.
Vol 3

Oct 15

Army Form C. 2118

WAR DIARY
or
INTELLIGENCE SUMMARY
(Erase heading not required.)

79th Brigade R.F.A.   Page 4

Place	Date	Hour	Summary of Events and Information	Remarks and references to Appendices
DICKEBUSCH	1/6 to 5/6		Normal Trench Warfare. No incidents of any importance to record	—
	3rd	8.0 p.m.	1 Section of 51st Brigade R.F.A. relieved a section of each battery of the 79 Brigade R.F.A.	—
	5th	8.0 p.m.	Remaining section relieved. Command of LEFT GROUP passed to O.C. 51st Brigade R.F.A. 79th Brigade R.F.A. (Colonel Carter) 9th Division withdrew to waggon lines near BOESCHEPE and RENNINGHELST. During period 79 Brigade was in action only two slight casualties occurred which did not necessitate either man leaving duty.	—
	6th	1.0 p.m.	79 Brigade R.F.A. marched to near Lillers about St SYLVESTRE-CAPPEL. All units arrived before midnight.	—
	7th to 20th		Brigade Resting.	—
	18th		Major B. George KIRKER left the Brigade on appointment to command 117th Brigade R.F.A. 28th Division.	—
			Captain C. HAMISR R.F.A. (transferred from A/80) took over command of B/79	—
	20th	7.30 a.m.	Advance Parties left ST SYLVESTRE-CAPPEL for KRUITSTRAAT to take over from units 42nd Brigade R.F.A. 3rd Division.	—
KRUITSTRAAT	23rd	8.0 p.m.	1 Section of each battery relieved section batteries 42nd Brigade R.F.A.	—
	24th	8.0 p.m.	Remaining sections relieved. Battery in action. Command of the Right group R.F.A. (Col. GEDDES C.B.) to O.C. 79th Brigade R.F.A. ("B" Col U.C. ANDERSON) The Right Group now consists of 79th Brigade R.F.A. and C/79	—

Army Form C. 2118

WAR DIARY or INTELLIGENCE SUMMARY

79 Brigade R.F.A. Page 5.

(Erase heading not required.)

Instructions regarding War Diaries and Intelligence Summaries are contained in F.S. Regs., Part II. and the Staff Manual respectively. Title Pages will be prepared in manuscript.

Place	Date	Hour	Summary of Events and Information	Remarks and references to Appendices
KRUITSTRAAT	25th	6 pm	79 A.B. relieved the 42nd B.A.C. The relief, Battery Positions, O.Ps and waggon lines are as follows.	Cu.
			Unit Position O.P. waggon lines	
			H.Q. 79 H.18.d.77	
			A/79 relieved H.Q. 42 " " C.16 c 6.3 3 men	
			B/79 " 1st Belgian Battery I.15.c.68 I.16.a.b8 C.18 a 8.8 A 4 b 7 8	
			C/79 " 24th Battery R.F.A. I.27 a b5 — — B 2 b 7 5	
			D/79 " 108th Battery R.F.A. I.15 a 30 J.13 c 5 D C.17 b 5.7 A 4 b 7 4	
			C/78 " 45th " I.27 b 53 2.0 b 56 C.22 b 87 A 9 b 8 1	Cu.
			" 109th " I.15 a 51 24 d 75 C.16 d 49 B 3 b 78	
			" I.15 a 61 10 c 31 C.24 b 10.8	
			BA/79 " 42nd BAC. — — C.14 a 2.5	
			O.C. 9/78 Capt HUMPHREYS R.F.A.	
	26th to 30th		Normal Trench Warfare. Nothing of any importance to record. Thirtiferious man gun in registering. 3 men. Gun man slightly wounded.	Cu. Cu.

Cochrane Lt Col R.F.A.
Commanding 79 Brigade R.F.A.
3.11.1915

79th Bde. BM.
Vol. 4
121/7634

14th Warwicks

Nov 15

WAR DIARY or INTELLIGENCE SUMMARY

Army Form C. 2118

79th Brigade R.F.A. — Page 6

(Erase heading not required.)

Place	Date	Hour	Summary of Events and Information	Remarks and references to Appendices
KRUISTRAAT	5th Nov / 6 Nov		Normal Trench Warfare. Nothing of importance to record. Weather very wet.	—
	6 Nov	6.0 AM / 6.30 AM	Lt Col WILLIS took over temporary command of RIGHT GROUP during the absence of Col PREOLONEL ON DESIGN. Combined shoot with Heavy Group and 60th Brigade R.F.A. Group, 9th Division on enemy front line trench and communication trench. Behind 6.0am — 6.30am. Ammunition used 40 A 90 HE for battery. Very little retaliation.	—
	7th Nov	12 noon to 4.0 pm	YPRES and battery positions of Group heavily shelled from most distant 4 gun retaliation given. No casualties within the battalion of the group.	—
	8th Nov	10.0 AM to 10.25 AM	Continued shoot with Heavy Group on enemy trenches. Enemy retaliated with concentrated fire on B1, B2 & B3 Nyonite trenches. Enemy retaliation on gun positions on YPRES late at night. Are men of A/79 wounded.	—
	9th Nov	2.0 pm	1 Section of each battery relieved by section of 52 F.F.A.s 9th Division. Sections which have been relieved within turn relieve section of 14th Division. Three men A/79 Brigade killed by shell fire during the day.	—
	10th Nov		Quiet. Very fine.	—
	11th Nov	12.30pm	Very wet. 3 men O/79 killed.	—
		8.30pm	Remaining sections of 79th F.F.A.s relieved by sections 52 F.F.A.s. Commanded by E Ayr Jones from Lt Col WILLIS to Lt Col PERREAU. Sections 79 F.F.A.s and C/79 complete relief of returns 14 Division. Command of Group hands over from Lt Col PERREAU D.S.O. to Lt Col WILLIS. Group so now known as LEFT GROUP 17 DIVISION ARTILLERY.	—
YPRES (DIXMUDE GATE)		10.0pm	GROUP 17 DIVISION ARTILLERY	—

WAR DIARY or INTELLIGENCE SUMMARY

79th Brigade R.F.A., Page 7

Army Form C. 2118

Place	Date	Hour	Summary of Events and Information	Remarks and references to Appendices
YPRES (MENIN GATE)	14th March		Col ANDERSON returned from leave and took over command of the LEFT GROUP	Cu.
	11th to 21st		Time was spent in registering etc. Hostile artillery fairly active, burning two gun pits. Counter battery was carried out on roads. Casualties during this period. A/79 2 wounded. B/79 1 wounded. C/79 1 killed 4 wounded. D/79 1 wounded. Total 2 killed 9 wounded. There was some change in the group. A/79 going over to the RIGHT GROUP and D/78 and D/79 coming into the LEFT GROUP. The final disposition of the group was as follows	Cu. Cu. Cu. Cu.
			Reference map Sheet 28 N.E. 1/10,000	

Sub group	Bty	Position	Covering Trenches	Normal Zone	Maximum Zone
Right	D/79	I.2.d.25	H.11 to H.7	I.12.c.93 — I.12.c.59	J.13.c.39 — I.5.b.84
"	B/79	I.2.b.35	H.13 to H.9	I.12.c.69 — I.12.c.24	I.12.c.93 — I.6.c.70
Right Counter Bty	D/78	I.1.d.10	H.11 to H.9	I.12.c.93 — I.12.c.24	J.19.c.67 — I.6.c.35
Left	C/79	I.3.c.54	H.9 to H.6.1	I.12.c.24 — I.12.a.08	I.12.c.86 — I.6.c.9
"	A/78	I.2.d.39	H.9 to H.6.1	I.12.a.08 — I.6.c.12	I.18.c.10 — I.6.c.19
Left Counter Bty	A/78	I.2.d.10	H.9 to H.6.1	I.12.c.24 — I.6.c.12	J.13.c.22 — I.6.c.09

Group Headquarters at I.1.b.72

WAR DIARY
or
INTELLIGENCE SUMMARY

79th BDE R.F.A. Page 8

Army Form C. 2118

(Erase heading not required.)

Instructions regarding War Diaries and Intelligence Summaries are contained in F. S. Regs., Part II. and the Staff Manual respectively. Title Pages will be prepared in manuscript.

Place	Date	Hour	Summary of Events and Information	Remarks and references to Appendices
YPRES (DIXMUDE RMR)	22nd to 30th		During this period. Nothing of importance to report. Of anything has been considerably more artillery activity	Clear
	29th	7.30pm	CAPT STUDDY and CAPT HUMPHREYS C/79 both went sick with nervous breakdown.	Clear

C.J.Churcher
Captain
Adjutant 79 F.A.B.
30/4/15.

79th Bde: R.F.A.
fol: 5

121/7931

17/2/21

WAR DIARY
INTELLIGENCE SUMMARY

79TH BDE. R.F.A.

Page 9

Army Form C. 2118

Place	Date	Hour	Summary of Events and Information	Remarks and references to Appendices
YPRES (DIXMUDE GATE)	1915 Dec 4th		Normal Trench Warfare	
	5th	7.30pm	Normal day. 1 man C/79 wounded	
	6th	10.00am	" " 2Lt DOBINSON C/79 wounded.	
	7th		Normal day. Nothing to note	
	8th		" "	
	9th	9.0am	Command of LEFT GROUP passes from O.C. 79TH F.A. (COL. W.E. ANDERSON) to O.C. 18TH F.A.B. (LT COL WILLIS). Headquarters 79TH F.A.B. relieved by Headquarters 78TH F.A.B. Headquarters acting Brigade attached to LEFT GROUP. War diaries now being kept by batteries.	
	9th to 12th			
	13th		COL. W.E. ANDERSON evacuated sick. MAJOR WARREN assumes temporary command of the Brigade.	
	13th 14th		Resting. CAPT C.P.N ARJANI temporarily attached to D/80 on 13th in CAPT BUCHAN who takes over duty of adjutant 79 Bde., on night 15th—16th December CAPT MARSHALL late of staff captain 79 F.A.B again.	
	15th			
	19th		Temp LT COL R.W. CATTLE R.G.A. in place to command 79 F.A.B. vice COL W.E. ANDERSON evacuated	
	18th		to England.	

WAR DIARY
INTELLIGENCE SUMMARY

Army Form C. 2

99⁹ F A Bde. Page 10

Place	Date	Hour	Summary of Events and Information	Remarks and references to Appendices
YPRES	19²	5:40 am	Enemy made a Gas attack on the front immediately north of 1 de Zne	18/1
			Inhalation 8/19. 1 Killed (12104 Gnr Willis CH)	19/1
	20⁵		Heavy shelling throughout day. Many Gas shells.	
	21⁵		A/19. 1 M&O badly injured (24053 Arpel C Appleby)	20/1
	24⁵		A/19 Batty Eatin shelled with about 50 77mm shells	21/1
	25⁵		Christmas Day. Normal	24/1
	26⁵		A/19 heavily shelled with 4.2 & 5.2 (about 100 Kds)	25/1
	29⁵		14 British Aeroplanes observed passing over Battener going East	26/1
	30⁵		Normal Trench Warfare	29/1
	31⁵			

Army Form C. 2118

WAR DIARY
or
INTELLIGENCE SUMMARY
(Erase heading not required.)

Instructions regarding War Diaries and Intelligence Summaries are contained in F. S. Regs., Part II. and the Staff Manual respectively. Title Pages will be prepared in manuscript.

Place	Date	Hour	Summary of Events and Information	Remarks and references to Appendices
YPRES			Normal trench Warfare	
			Brigade relieved by 106th Brigade 24th A.D. 24th Div.	
			Brigade in Rest Billets at Lumeghem. Training being carried out.	

79th Bde: R.F.A.
Vol: 6

17

17

79th Bde: R.F.A.
Vol: 7

WAR DIARY or INTELLIGENCE SUMMARY

Army Form C. 2118

1st Sheet

Place	Date Feb.	Hour	Summary of Events and Information	Remarks and references to Appendices
TOURNEHEM	1 to 4		Bde in Rest Billets at TOURNEHEM. Training carried out under Divisional and Brigade Arrangements.	
"	5		Bgde marched from TOURNEHEM to STEENVOORDE arriving about 5pm. 6" Feb.	
STEENVOORDE	6		A, B & C/79 relieved 1st Sections of 107, 109 & 108 Battys respectively	
"	7		2nd " " " " "	
OOREBUSCH	8		D/79 take over three forward Guns from 23rd Bde D/79 remaining Gun attached to C/79	
"	9	7pm	Command of RIGHT GROUP passed from OC 23rd Bde R.F.A. to OC 79th Bde R.F.A. RIGHT GROUP 17th Div consisting of:- (SHEET 28).	

Unit	No. of Guns		MAP REFERENCE
A/79	4	18 PRs	#35 a.3.8
B/79	"	"	#35 c.1.5
C/79	5	"	#28 d.4.½
D/79	3	Single Guns	I28c32 I33a.19 I33a3.½
D/81	2	4·5" How	N.4.c.9.7.

	10 to 13		Registration carried out by Batteries. Situation normal.	
	14			
	15	5pm	Enemy attack on our left causing some artillery activity on our front. Fanatic attack made on enemy occupying front taken previous evening. RIGHT GROUP did not participate	

WAR DIARY or INTELLIGENCE SUMMARY

Army-Form C. 2118

(Erase heading not required.)

Place	Date Feb.	Hour	Summary of Events and Information	Remarks and references to Appendices
DICKEBUSCH	16		Situation normal.	
	17			
	18		B/79 R/79 attached to 5th Bde R.F.A. (Lahore Div Artillery). D/81 Bring 1.4.5" Howitz action	
	19		6 Batty R.F.A. & 69 Batty R.F.A. came into action to form front of Right Group (Mob.c.92.E).	
			6 Batty act # 84 c umb h. 9 ? at N 5 a 3 8.	
	20			
	21		Situation normal	
	22		Retaliation called for at intervals by Infantry.	
	23			
	24		Severe weather experienced from 24th. (Snow)	
	25			
	26			
	27		All Batteries in Group fairly active with Retaliation requested by Infantry.	
	28		Casualty 1 Officer Lieut +C.A. LITCHFIELD D/79 wounded 5pm	
	29		27th 2.28th. Severe Weather continues	

79 RFA
Vol 8

Army Form C. 2118

WAR DIARY
or
INTELLIGENCE SUMMARY
(Erase heading not required.)

79th BRIGADE R.F.A.   Page 3

Place	Date MARCH	Hour	Summary of Events and Information	Remarks and references to Appendices
DICKEBUSCH	1st		Retaliation by Infantry Request at intervals by All Batteries.	Apl.
"	"	5-10pm	Demonstration by all All Batteries under Div. Orders on Areas	*4·5 Hows
		5.05pm	in support of attack on the BLUFF (N. of CANAL & N.E. of ST ELOI) Pg 17-Div.	
			D/81 *(2 Guns) 0.2.d.28 - 35 - 4.7	
			D/81 *(1 Gun) 0.2.d.33 - 4.4 - 7.4	
			A/79 (2 Guns) 0.2.d.17 - 0.2.d. 74	
			C/79 Batty (4 Guns) 0.2.a.74 - 0.3.c.4!	
			B/79 Batty 0.2.c.73 - 9.2 - 10.4 - 9.6	
			Casualties	
			Capt W.N. Gillum D/79 Wounded 5.30pm 1st March	
			but at hostile b/79 Slightly at duty 5.30pm 1st March	
			R.O. i/c A/79	
			58907 Serjt J.W. Green D/79 ⎫	
			33363 Bomb D. Pearman " ⎬ Wounded	
			58135 Gunner W Howe " ⎪	
			38214 Gunner R Hamilton " ⎭	
2nd		6:30am	Assault made by our Infantry on "Bluff". 81st Group did not participate in preliminary bombardment, 2 forward Guns of D/79 damaged.	Apl.
3rd			Enemy artillery active. All Batteries Retaliate during day.	Apl.

WAR DIARY / INTELLIGENCE SUMMARY

79th BRIGADE R.F.A. Army Form C. 2118

Page 4

Place	Date	Hour	Summary of Events and Information	Remarks and references to Appendices
DICKEBUSCH	4.		Normal Trench Warfare.	A91
"	5.		"	A91
"	6.		"	A91
"	7.		"	A91
"	8.	5pm	C/79 Bdr took over ground covered by 6th Batty 6th Batty going to Canadian Group.	A91
"	9.		Normal Trench Warfare.	A91
"	10.		Single Gun D/81 withdrawn to Wagon lines	A91
"	11.	2am		
		8pm	Section D/81 relieved by Section 130 Batty / 2 Single Guns of D/79 taken over by 45th Batty.	A91
"	12.	9am to 9.45	1st Sections of all Batteries move off from Wagon Lines into Gun & Gun Personnel & march to PRADELLE area.	A91
"		9.45	1st Sections A/79 B/79 C/79 relieved by 1st Sections 107 & 108 Battys respectively	A91
"	12	6pm	1st Section A/79 B/79 C/79 relieved by 1st Sections 107, 107, 108 Batty respectively	A91
"	13	9am	2nd Section all Batteries Hdqrs - B&C move H.J. from Dug-Out Lines & march to PRADELLES	A91
"	"	9.45am	"	
"		6pm	2nd Sections A/79 B/79 C/79 relieved by 2nd Section 108, 107 & 108 Battys respectively.	A91
"			Forward of Right Group passed from OC 79 Div R.F.A to OC 25th Div R.F.A.	A91
"			Personnel in Gun Positions carried to PRADELLES on nights of 12/13 13/14 by Motor Lorry.	A91
PRADELLES	14.		Bde in Billets at PRADELLES.	A91
"	15.		"	A91
"	16.		Batty Commandant & O forward to Reconnoitre Positions near ARMENTIERES & troops & Coys A91	

WAR DIARY
or
INTELLIGENCE SUMMARY

79th BRIGADE R.F.A. Army Form C. 2118

Page 5

Place	Date	Hour	Summary of Events and Information	Remarks and references to Appendices
PRADELLES	16		Advance Party consisting 1 Officer 2 Telephonists (2) forward from HQ B/79 & C/79	A.9.1
"	17		Bde Commander & Comd forward to Reconnoitre new Battery Positions	A.9.1
"	18	9am	1st Sections B/79 & C/79 move off from PRADELLES to relieve 1st Sections of B/95 & C/95 respectively in ARMENTIERES area.	A.9.1
"		9.15am		A.9.1
"	19	9am	2nd Sections B/79, C/79 move off from PRADELLES to relieve 2nd Sections of B/95 & C/95 respectively.	A.9.1
"		9.15am		A.9.1
"	20	9.0am	Advance parties of A/79 & D/79 go forward to reconnoitre Bde HQ & wns of A/79 from PRADELLES & relieve 95 Bde A/C	A.9.1
		9.30am	Situation normal. Pages A/79, D/79 out PRADELLES	A.9.1
	21st			A.9.1
	22nd	9.0am	First Sections of A/79, D/79 march to ARMENTIERES Area relieve 1st sections A/95 & D/95 respectively	A.9.1
ARMENTIERES	23rd	9.15am	Second Sections of A/79 & D/79 march to ARMENTIERES Area & relieve 2nd sections A/95 & D/95 respectively	A.9.1
		9.0am		
		9.15am		
		12.0mn	Command of LEFT GROUP passed from A/95 > D/95 to 95 Bde RFA to OC 79 Bde RFA	A.9.1

LEFT GROUP comprises
A/79   1 Sec: C.20.d.24   1 Sec C.20.d.66.
B/79   C.25.b.4.6.
C/79   C.14.c.9.2.
D/79   1 Sec C.22.a.35   1 Sec C.27.a.5.3.
2/51   C.20.c.8.8.

A.9.1

Army Form C. 2118

WAR DIARY
or
INTELLIGENCE SUMMARY
(Erase heading not required.)

HEADQUARTERS 9TH BRIGADE R.F.A.

79th BRIGADE, R.F.A. Page 6

Place	Date March	Hour	Summary of Events and Information	Remarks and references to Appendices
ARMENTIERES	24th	—	Registration by all Batteries. Situation normal.	
"	25th		Normal day. Batteries registering	
"	26th		C/79 withdrew from their position after dark, and move to new position at H.24.c.28 (Sheet 36) to reinforce 34th Division to stop the	CMC
"		5.30pm	gap attached temporarily for tactical purposes. A,B,&D batteries under their own and B/79 took over previously covered by C.	CMC
"	27th 28th 29th		Normal Trench warfare.	
"	30th	"		
"	31st	"	2nd Lieut. A.M. Ludovici and 2nd Lieut. H.F. Wilmott joined the Brigade and were posted to B and C Batteries respectively.	CMC

D.W. Custis
Lt.Col.
Comm. 79th Bde. R.F.A.

Army Form C. 2118

Vol 9
Page 7

XVI

WAR DIARY
or
INTELLIGENCE SUMMARY
(Erase heading not required.)

79th Bde R.F.A.

Place	Date April	Hour	Summary of Events and Information	Remarks and references to Appendices
ARMENTIERES	1st	10am 11am	Enemy Artillery unusually active. Some 200 shells, 7.7cm, 10.5cm, 11.8cm fired ut & 1100 PLUMER during course of morning. Trench Mortars B/79 30/e1 fired 80.30m. "H E" at Tilleloy. Normal day.	CM.C
	2nd		Reported the flag of a hostile airplane carried a/c by B/79.	CM.C
	3rd		2 Officers and 30 men of 2nd Australian Division attached to us today. All proceedings to B/79. Demon for same.	CM.C
	4th 5th 6th 7th 8th 9th		Ordre received CRA re mutual assistance between artilleries of 9th Division & on our left. Zone for "BARRAGE LEFT" altered to a line N.E. Batteries registered targets for above.	CM.C CM.C CM.C
	10th 11th		Normal trench warfare. Some registration carried on with Relaxation scheme. Order issued and passed Battr'ies "No ammunition of any nature to be expended until further orders except for a change of line and agreed instructions of 2nd Australian Divison."	CM.C CM.C
	12th 13th 14th 15th 16th		do do do Seams stopped and all officers seen on line reported by 18th.	CM.C CM.C

WAR DIARY or INTELLIGENCE SUMMARY

Army Form C. 2118

Page 8.

79th Bde R.F.A.

Place	Date April	Hour	Summary of Events and Information	Remarks and references to Appendices
ARMENTIERES	17th		Normal trench warfare. Enemy artillery activity rather on the increase.	C.M.C.
	18th		Enemy shelled front line and support trenches between 8.10-11 am. About 80 rounds. No retaliation was asked for.	C.M.C.
	19th		"	
	20th		"	
	21st		"	
	22nd		Batteries ordered to register "gaps" in our front line trenches. Registration carried out.	C.M.C.
			Orders issued from 87 D.A. that ammunition of all natures could now be fired. No retaliation. Expenditure the limits asked for a provide.	
	23rd		C/79 relieved by 13th Battery Australian F.A., the 34th Div. having been relieved by 2nd Australian Div. Personnel & wagon lines of	C.M.C.
			7 horses killed and 4 injured by hostile Anti-aircraft shell dropping in A/79 wagon lines.	
	24th	10am	C/91 ordered to engage hostile battery reported active at O.18 K.77. 20 rds 9.45	C.M.C.
	25th		C/79 re-occupied old (position at C.14d.12. after dark	
	26th		C/79 reported being in position morning	
		3:0pm	Bombardment of PONT BALLOT Salient by RIGHT GROUP & HARVARD Sector DION (vide D/79) and C/91 ordered to fire few of trench mortars opposite trenches 8 and 29. Remainder of group to be in readiness to reply to hostile retaliation fire.	C.M.C.
		5:30pm	Hostile bombardment started on trenches 8 and 9 but LEFT GROUP D/50, D/79, A/91, A/56 C/91 ordered to fire 20 rds in retaliation on trench 58.	
		5:40		
		5:50	A/79, B/79, D/79, D/50 and C/91 ordered to fire "Retaliation A" (support & CM trenches)	
		5:55	Continue until further notice. Batteries ordered to open chlorine & expend four rounds	C.M.C.

1875 Wt. W593/826 1,000,000 4/15 I.B.C. & A. A.D.S.S./Forms/C. 2118.

WAR DIARY or INTELLIGENCE SUMMARY

Army Form C. 2118

Page 9. 79½ Bde R.F.A.

Place	Date April	Hour	Summary of Events and Information	Remarks and references to Appendices
ARMENTIERES	26th (cont)	6.15	D/79 fired in to salient C17 a 43. D/80 on left line opposite Hitler 88 c 89	
		6.30	B/79 fired bursts of neutralisation to trench 87 a 88. A/79 "Retaliation A" (sprinkler)	
		6.30	How. Bg. of CENTRE GROUP on to Front trench opposite 87 a 88	
		6.35	C/81 kept up firing Section Fire. B/80 accurate	
		6.43	B/79 one action opposite "EDMEADS FARM"	
		7.07	C/81 & D/79 reports all quiet and that they had stopped firing	
		7.10	We wanted SOS RA all quiet we have stopped firing.	
		7.30pm	Hostile Bombardment on period without intensity. All batteries retaliated again	
		7.45	All batteries ordered to send "Retaliation A"	
		7.35	Slow rate of fire ordered. Found Germans in	
		8.15	Three reports received by A.D. Batteries. Started barrage fire	
		8.25	Germans reported to have entered trench 88, infantry now outside to by B/79 telephone. Fire flying over the only wire left. K front line Trench (104 wire losing) Germans reported kept up with Ken Batts. No fog this morning, gunners & Duke of Wellington on left, infantry trouble Sqd. and 2/9 communication with O.P.s kept on	
		8.30	D/79 went out as fire at F Section, buffer trouble.	
		8.40	B/79 about to start retaliation opposite trench 88. Brigade Major asked if	
			D/79 was wanted on trench 88. Replied that they were not.	
		8.45	Reported all quiet on front. Batteries stopped firing.	
		9.30	Communications with O.P.s restored. Reported that been shelled all night. He casualties and Gas shells. All main outs in NO FOXES caught my guard.	

WAR DIARY
or
INTELLIGENCE SUMMARY

(Erase heading not required.)

79th Bde R.F.A.

Page 10.

Army Form C. 2118

Place	Date	Hour	Summary of Events and Information	Remarks and references to Appendices
ARMENTIERES	April 1916 27th	2 am	D/79 reported all guns in action again. Today normal. C/79 carried out abt 20 rounds registration (One round) per calibre gun registration as follows:- C/79 (extreme right of Group) C.29.a.95 to C.23.c.98 B/79 (right centre) C.23.c.98 to C.23.b.48 A/79 (left centre) C.23.b.48 to C.17.c.89 D/79 (extreme left of Group) C.17.c.89 to C.17.a.07½ D/79 was ordered to keep watch. Battery moved about 300 x behind FRELINGHIEN. Also	CMC
		12.30 pm		CMC
	28th	3pm	C/81 was ordered to keep normal trench warfare	
	29th	"	2nd Lt C.H. Payton joined Brigade and reported to D/79.	CMC
	30th	"	Small bombardment of new trench enemy was digging in front of trenches 86, 87, 88 was arranged for 11.30 am A/79	
		11.20	D/79 + C/81 taking part. 18 pdrs 40 rounds. 4.5 hows 16 rounds.	

DW Curtis
Lt Col
Commdg 79 Bde R.F.A.

To Officer i/c A.G's Office.
　　　　Base.
　　　　―――――

Herewith war Diary for
May 1916, of 79th Bde R.F.A.

(?) IV Curtis

2/6/16
　　　　Lieut Colonel
　　　Commandg 79th Bde R.F.A.

Army Form C. 2118

Vol 10
Page 11.

WAR DIARY
or
INTELLIGENCE SUMMARY
(Erase heading not required.)

XVII
79th Bde R.F.A.

Instructions regarding War Diaries and Intelligence Summaries are contained in F.S. Regs, Part II. and the Staff Manual respectively. Title Pages will be prepared in manuscript.

Place	Date May 1916	Hour	Summary of Events and Information	Remarks and references to Appendices
ARMENTIERES	1.	12.5 am	Shots on new German trench started at 11.20 pm & repeated by A & D/79 & C/81	C.H.C.
		1.20 "	Shots again repeated – 18 pdr batteries 20 rds, this time 8 rounds each time.	C.H.C.
	1/2	12 midnight	Dud bugle shot on new trench was a repeated	
	2.	2.05 am	"	
	1	3.15 pm	C/79 Billet at Gunn poster shelled and turret blown proved. No casualties thereover. Considerable amount of equipment lost (but other YCRA attending to it.) That other YCRA attending (signals)	C.H.C.
	2	12.45	Brigade Retaliation 'A' (all batteries fired low trench) do do (signals)	
		1.30	do	
	3	-	Normal day.	
	4	-	Normal trench warfare.	
	5	10.15 am	92800 Gunner Lewis C/79 wounded slightly	C.H.C.
			Retaliation 'B' (on Enemy Support Trenches) at Infantry request at 10.15 am. All batteries of Left Group participated. A/79 & C/81 ordered to fire on rest enemy trench in C/17d. as above. Repeated at 12.45 am.	C.H.C.
	6	12.45 am		
	5–	6.30 pm	Heavy bombardment of CENTRE GROUP Front and to South of this. SOS. completed up by Divisions on Right. 3 Gas alarms sounded. All guns of LEFT Group front, group did not take part in counter bombardment.	C.H.C.
	6	"	Normal trench warfare	
	7	2.30 am	3 B/79 ordered to fire on new battle trench in C/17.d. 2 salvos each time	C.H.C.
	8	3.40 am	"	
	9		5 & 4 officers & other ranks of 3rd N.Z. Brigade F.A. attached to Left Group for instructional purposes	C.H.C.

Army Form C. 2118

WAR DIARY
or
INTELLIGENCE SUMMARY
(Erase heading not required.)

79th Bde R.F.A.   Page 12

Place	Date May 1916	Hour	Summary of Events and Information	Remarks and references to Appendices
ARMENTIERES	10		Normal Trench Warfare. Brigade Ammunition Column disbanded as from this day on reorganization of F.A. Brigades	CMC
	11		"	
	12		"	CMC
	13	6 a.m.	" Details of late Brigade Am. Col. left for Base (CALAIS)	
		7.15 p.m.	Forward Sect. D/79 (under 9th DIV) ordered to open fire on trenches opposite LE TOUQUET. X.F. 20"	
		7.28 "	Rate of Fire increased to X.F. 10". Rear section commenced "BARRAGE LEFT"	
		7.31 "	B/79 ordered 1 sect. "BARRAGE LEFT" X.F. one minute.	CMC
		7.45 "	B/79 and D/79. "Cease firing." Enemy trench on 9th DIV front not repaired	
	14		"	
	15		"	
	16		"	CMC
	17	12 noon	No 21093. Gr Derrigan M. A/79 slightly wounded. Shrapnel	
		11 p.m.	79th Bde RFA relieved by 3rd Bde NZFA. A/79 Section shelled, shelter destroyed	CMC
VIEUX BERQUIN	18	12.15pm	Bde marched to billets at VIEUX BERQUIN	
RENESCURE	19	11 a.m.	" from VIEUX BERQUIN to RENESCURE	
NIELLES-LEZ-BLEQUIN	20		" RENESCURE to NIELLES LEZ-BLEQUIN	
BLEQUIN	21		Brigade billeted in Training Area. Day devoted to cleaning up & billeting down	
	22		Intensive Training began, under Battery arrangements. {Under Artillery Brigade Reorgan etc. D/79 became B/81 and C/81 formed 79th Bde as 4.5" How battery, now	CMC
	23		" " continued	
	24		"	
	25		" known as D/79}	

Army Form C. 2118

WAR DIARY
or
INTELLIGENCE SUMMARY
(Erase heading not required.)

79th Bde R.F.A.   Page 13

Place	Date	Hour	Summary of Events and Information	Remarks and references to Appendices
NIELLES-LEZ-BLEQUIN	May 26		Intense Training continued under Brigade Arrangements	A.W.C.
	27		" " " " " "	
	28		" " " under Divisional Arrangements	A.W.C.
	29		" " " " " "	
	30		" " " " " "	
	31		" " " " " "	

A W McLeod
Lieutenant Colonel
Command? 79th Bde R.F.A.

WAR DIARY or INTELLIGENCE SUMMARY

Army Form C. 2118

79th Bde. R.F.A.

Vol 11. Page 13

June

Place	Date June	Hour	Summary of Events and Information	Remarks and references to Appendices
NIELLES-LEZ-BLEQUIN	1		Intense Training continued under Divisional Arrangements	CMC
	2		" " " " " "	
	3,4,5		" " " " " "	
	6,7,8,9		" " " " " "	
THEROUANNE	10	8pm	Brigade marched to THEROUANNE and bivouacked for following day	
WAVRANS	11	8.30pm	" " " NAVRANS " " "	CMC
NEUVILLETTE	12	8 pm	" " " NEUVILLETTE " " "	
TALMAS	13	8.30pm	" " " TALMAS " " "	
HEILLY	14	9 pm	" " " HEILLY " " "	
VILLE-SOUS-CORBIE	15	3.30pm	" " " VILLE-SOUS-CORBIE and occupied wagon lines	CMC
CORBIE	16		2.10 Div Art and A of D field by 9th Bde RFA. B/79 Reconnts new postn & B/79 good. C attn taking up positn from 96 Bde RFA (C. F.19.b.55. Map Sheet 62D) attached to 9th Bde RFA.	
	17	4pm	A&C/79 preparing new positns. D/79 (How) attached to 78th Bde RFA.	CMC
		11am	No 53448 Bdr Cross B HQ staff wounded in MEAULTE by hostile Anti-aircraft shell, shot 21662 Gnr Sturgeon " " burst preman in magazine. 21 new field. 21.9128 Gnr Egerton on ZA/79 wounded all positn, bullet	
	18	night	A & C/79 batteries took up new positns. Preparatory bombardment of importance by enemy ten hds dead at all	CMC
	19	night	Note no gun positns of all batteries on Branch	
	20		" " " " " "	
	21	3am	Gnr Clarkson 9 A/79 wounded at gun positn snipers bullet.	
	22		Work on Gun positns continued	
BECOURT-BECORDEL	23	6pm	Bde HQ moved up to Forward HQ. Communications established, batteries in action by 6pm	CMC
	24	4.30am	Preliminary bombardment started. 9th Bde + on/by B of 79th Bde engaged. Weather dull all day also D/79 attached 57 & 18 Bde	

WAR DIARY
or
INTELLIGENCE SUMMARY

79th Bde R.F.A.   Page 13

Army Form C. 2118

Place	Date June	Hour	Summary of Events and Information	Remarks and references to Appendices
BECOURDEL	24	10am	Casualties (No 44858 Sergt Britten W) (Since died of wounds) 4722 Corpl Jones ST. 1287 Gnr Searle G. Wounded by premature at gun muzzle. 46644 . Yeatly C	C.M.C.
	25	9pm	No 21136 Gnr Hunt wounded slightly. Gas shell 4.2 cm. No 45507 Sgt A Winwood D/NC. Wippes de Shott. Bombardment continued. Wire cutting all day.	C.M.C.
	26	9.00	Intense Bombardment by 20 minutes on BOTTOM WOOD. Gas shell onto Left of Sultzer's redoubt. The 3.5 mm. Wire cutting continued all day. Concentrated Bombardment on Sunk lane & support trenches at 3.0 & 4.30 pm	C.M.C.
		11.30am	"	C.M.C.
	27		— — — assault postponed — — —	
	28			
	29	6.30pm	No 96303 Gnr Moberley SPG slightly wounded head	C.M.C.
	30		Wire cutting continued all day. Intense bombardment of Enemy positions 8.00 am to 9.20 am	

D W Curtis
Lieut Colonel
Commanding 79th Bde R.F.A.

17th Div.
XV. Corps.

WAR DIARY

Headquarters,

79th BRIGADE, R.F.A.

J U L Y

1 9 1 6

17bis

WAR DIARY or INTELLIGENCE SUMMARY

Army Form C. 2118

79th Bde. R.F.A. — Page 14.

Place	Date July	Hour	Summary of Events and Information	Remarks and references to Appendices
BÉCORDEL	1	6.25	Heavy bombardment of enemy lines commenced.	
		7.30	Bombardment lifted & our Infantry attack commenced.	
		7.45	A/79 reports Infantry line that find lines that only portion was taken.	
		8.00	Infantry reported advance beyond support trench and entire of SUNKEN ROAD by ROUND WOOD.	
		8.50	Our Infantry reported N. of PEAR WOOD. 50th Bde. reported held up by M.G. fire from	
		9.20	Cruxifix Trench & KONIG TRENCH.	
		9.30	Infantry report S. of SUNKEN ROAD for line (tanks) of FRICOURT WOOD	
		11.30	Infantry report infilade and M.G. fire from BOTTOM WOOD & X.28.d. 64 (Sheet 57c)	
			A & C/79 ordered to establish Barrage on RAIL Trench running from	
			MAMETZ & MONTAUBAN reported captured by Divisions on our left & right	
		1pm	Lines all round slackened.	
		2pm	Bombardment of FRICOURT ordered. Repulsed at 2.30 by attack. This was not successful	CMC
		3pm	Own Infantry now held line ROUND WOOD, SUNKEN ROAD, LOZENGE WOOD & ALLEY, POODLES, CRUCIFIX	
			TRENCH, THE DINGLE	
		9.40pm	4 Div. Artillery of our neighbourhood of LOZENGE WOOD. Heavy German bombardment.	
			Batteries opened rapid slow attack line. No Infantry counter attack followed.	
	2	11pm	Heavy fire had stopped. Batteries rate to fire regular per hour on the E. & N. on front portion	CMC
		9.15am	Ordered Brigade bombardment line. Infantry to Bombardment and attack of FRICOURT opened.	
			Cancelled at Second portable Ptl.t. Germans had withdrawn from front line here.	
		12.30pm	57th Ind. Bde. occupied FRICOURT and cleared FRICOURT WOOD, & occupied FRICOURT FARM.	
		3.0pm	Infantry now holding line ROUND WOOD, CRUCIFIX TRENCH, FRICOURT FARM, part of RAILWAY ALLEY	
			to N.E. corner of FRICOURT WOOD – joining with 7th Div. on right at WILLOW TRENCH.	
		9.0pm	Night reconnaissance along line S.E. corner of SHELTER WOOD. S.J.7 BOTTOM WOOD, RAILWAY COPSE	
			to RAILWAY ALLEY X.29.c.63	
			Bombardment ordered of line RAILWAY ALLEY, East of X.29. c.63, RAILWAY COPSE, BOTTOM WOOD.	
	3	8.40am	SHELTER WOOD, BIRCH TREE WOOD. 21st Div. SHELTER & BIRCH TREE WOOD.	CMC
		9.0am	17th Div. attack RAILWAY ALLEY, RAILWAY COPSE & BOTTOM WOOD. QUADRANGLE TRENCH, WOOD TRENCH, QUADRANGLE SUPPORT and STRIP TRENCH	
		9.30am	Artillery fire Weak – QUADRANGLE TRENCH, WOOD TRENCH, QUADRANGLE SUPPORT and STRIP TRENCH	
			Infantry signalled (C/79 "Stopping on Quadrangle, ordered right and left"	

Army Form C. 2118

WAR DIARY or INTELLIGENCE SUMMARY

79th Bde R.F.A. Page 18

(Erase heading not required.)

Place	Date July	Hour	Summary of Events and Information	Remarks and references to Appendices
BECORDEL	3	10 am	Quiet day. Little Artillery Activity. Batteries kept up desultory fire in "TRIP TRENCH" throughout day & 7.30 pm. Infantry gradually pushing in. Many prisoners taken. Infantry of 21st Div relieved by 17th Div in evening. Interview not issued.	CMC
	4	2 pm	A & C Batteries ordered to cut wire in front of QUADRANGLE SUPPORT TRENCH. Continued on this task during afternoon. B/79 preparing new position near A+C pit N of FRICOURT. 21st Infantry are now all relieved 3 Divs. Relieved by 17th Div.	CMC
	5	12.15 am	Bombardment of QUADRANGLE TRENCH started. 79th Batteries assisted. Attack on QUADRANGLE TRENCH by 52nd Inf. Bde. Successful.	
		12.45	S.O.S. QUADRANGLE TRENCH received from 2/2 A. A,B & C Batteries opened rate X fire, 15"	
		12.0 pm	Fire stopped.	
		12.35	A,B,C ordered to enfilade QUADRANGLE SUPPORT TRENCH and ACID DROP COPSE	
		4.0 pm	D/79 to shell MAMETZ WOOD from our line. A,B +C to keep up fire, 120 rds per hour on German Second line, North of MAMETZ wood, until daylight.	CMC
		10.30 pm		
	6	10 am	A & C Bombarded ACID DROP COPSE and CEMETERY for 20 minutes, X Fire 15".	
		1.40 pm	B + C " " " "	
		4.0 pm	A + B " " " "	
	7	1.25 am	Intense Bombardment of QUADRANGLE SUPPORT TRENCH all Batteries	
		2.0 am	Infantry Assault. Unsuccessful.	
		7.30 pm	Bombardment of QUADRANGLE SUPPORT TRENCH restarted	
		8.00 am	A & C on QUADRANGLE SUPPORT Bombardment turned on MAMETZ WOOD. All Batteries	
		8.30 am	Barrage across MAMETZ WOOD began to lift.	
		8.40	Our Infantry reported advancing on CONTALMAISON on SW side	
		10.0 a	Davas lifted off MAMETZ WOOD and on to German Second Line behind	
		12.30 pm	CONTALMAISON reported occupied by III Corps. ACID DROP COPSE, CEMETERY and one of QUADRANGLE SUPPORT TRENCH by 17th Division.	
		3.05 pm	D/79 ordered to shell near QUADRANGLE SUPPORT & ALLEY & MAMETZ WOOD & W. edge of latter	
		5.00 pm	CONTALMAISON reported evacuated by British Troops	CMC

WAR DIARY or INTELLIGENCE SUMMARY

Army Form C. 2118

79th Bde R.F.A. Page 16

Place	Date July	Hour	Summary of Events and Information	Remarks and references to Appendices
BECORDEL	7	11.30 pm	Night firing on German second line & field of battery at a time until 3:30 a.m.	
	8	4:30 a.m	D/79 attack K hole QUADRANGLE ALLEY to junction with QUADRANGLE Support, & battery it of Pearl <?>	
		7:00 a.m	Barrage attack upon QUADRANGLE SUPPORT. D/79 attack K hole QUAD. ALLEY. North'y SUPPORT	
		11:30 a.m	A, B acl batteries reduced the rep of trolley line (boyne on bathy pen lon) in western edge of MAMETZ WOOD	
			until 2:30 p.m. B also had in parts of its enemy entry of CONTALMAISON	
		5:25	Half hour bombardment, ACID DROP COPSE, QUADRANGLE ALLEY & MAMETZ WOOD all attack	C.M.C.
		5:50	Infantry looking attack QUADRANGLE SUPPORT re: Batteries barrage MAMETZ WOOD. Western edge.	
			high-firing started, on battery for 2 hours, 50 yds per hour leading into CONTALMAISON	
	9	11 pm	D/79 search fire in QUADRANGLE ALLEY until 12:15 am. B/79 sniping enemy battery CONTALMAISON in G.	
		11:15 a.m	Heavy bombardment of our front line, and on III Corps front on left, when infantry counter attack	
		1:00 pm	were also launched later. No infantry attack on 17th Div. front.	
		6 pm	Zone fire night firing on German second line from X 12 a 30 & S14 a 35 allotted to 79th Bde.	
			Batteries fired IL fire nightly from 10 pm to 4 am — in shifts 8 1½ hours per battery.	
		11:10 pm	Infantry attack on QUADRANGLE SUPPORT. 18 pdr. (A&B) batteries ordered barrage Western	
			edge of MAMETZ WOOD from X 23 b 58 & X 17 a 86 from 11:20 pm to 12:30 pm.	C.M.C.
	10	12:30 a.m	Above the pair battery at attached to carry on barrage until 3:30 a.m. Salvos at 5 min intervals.	
		3:30 a.m	Bombardment of MAMETZ WOOD started A & C on S.W. edge from X 30 a 12 to X 24 C 03	
			Band D on QUADRANGLE ALLEY North of junction with SUPPORT. 13 pdrs came into it until 4:15 am	
		4:15 a.m	Bombardment lifted gradually Northwards, reaching road Slowly at 5 pm.	
		8:15 a.m	Barrage lifted to German second line. MAMETZ WOOD removed in hands of our infantry	
		9:30 a.m	Much enemy movement reported from O.Ps. about CONTALMAISON VILLA and N.E. corner	
			of CONTALMAISON. Checked by heavy Artillery fire. 79th Bde Barrage from LOWER	
			NOSD to PEARL WOOD, between German second line & MAMETZ WOOD.	
		10 a.m	Batteries ordered to search back from above Barrage line, to behind German second line	C.M.C.

Army Form C. 2118

WAR DIARY
or
INTELLIGENCE SUMMARY

79th Bde R.F.A.   Page 17

(Erase heading not required.)

Place	Date	Hour	Summary of Events and Information	Remarks and references to Appendices
BECORDEL	July 10	5.45pm	To assist III Corps attack on CONTALMAISON 79th Brigade ordered to shell PEARL ALLEY from X.17.c.53 to vicinity of PEARL WOOD	C.M.C.
		7.10pm	III Corps having taken CONTALMAISON, all batteries ordered to lift barrage North of THE CUTTING, to prevent German reinforcements arriving to catch enemy retiring along PEARL ALLEY from X.17.a.17 to CUTTINGS and NORTHWARDS. 17.X.1.6.45 ordered open battery rate of fire 1 rnd pr battery per minute, units batteries.	
		9.20pm	Rate of Barrage quickened up to Section fire 30 seconds, enemy reported massing in PEARL ALLEY	
	11	12.0am	Barrage returned to original rate of fire, & kept up all morning to next day	
		3.0pm	A, C & D Batteries started to barrage German Second line, from S.14.a.35 to S.13.c.97½ and searching back behind this zone & as high as BAZENTIN-LE-PETIT WOOD. Continued fire 50 hds quickenup B/79 Released on PEARL ALLEY BARRAGE and took over zone of fire from X.17.d.2.18 to X.17.b.44	C.M.C.
		7.30pm	B/79 ordered to barrage PEARL ALLEY from X.17.a.93 to X.17.c.85. No fire to be made at cutting	
	12	10am	B/79 ordered to lift Barrage from PEARL ALLEY and to go on to Second line zone whole Brigade ... monopoly this task	
		8.45am	Reported that an Infantry ... attack to occupy tunnel leading West from CUTTING, PEARL WOOD and CONTALMAISON VILLA.	
		5.45pm	All batteries ordered to quicken up fire for 30 minutes and search forward through wood in their area	C.M.C.
	13		Fire on German second line and BAZENTIN-LE-PETIT kept up all day	
	14	3.20am	Assault on BAZENTIN-LE-PETIT, accompanied by gradually lifting barrage through wood. BAZENTIN-LE-PETIT, BAZENTIN-LE-GRAND & LONGUEVAL all easily taken	
		7.30am		
		7.45am	Brigade ordered to move forward to position of readiness S.E. of FRICOURT WOOD	
		3.0pm	Bdy H.Q. established at X.28.b.2. Batteries in action at following points:- A/79 at X.23.b.45. C and D/79 at X.23.a.70. B/79 remaining in action 15 B/79 remaining in Madeuve.	
	15	8.30am	Half Coum Fontainhan-de-MartinC.C., ...running to 8. MARTIN PUICH shatter A, C & D/79 into park	C.M.C.

WAR DIARY or INTELLIGENCE SUMMARY

Army Form C. 2118

79th Bde R.F.A.

Page 8

Place	Date July	Hour	Summary of Events and Information	Remarks and references to Appendices
FRICOURT	15	9.8am	Batteries fell on MARTINPUICH village	C.M.C.
		11.5am	Barrage lifted to beyond MARTINPUICH	
		12.20 -	Batteries ordered to turn defensive bursts on MARTINPUICH West Pt. S Lois H.20' M 32 central.	
		2.0 pm	B/79 ordered to turn other section alongside first. In action at 5 pm.	
			No 20937 Gnr Sch. C. B/79 wounded.	
	16	10.0am	Brigade turned on German switch trench from S.33.c.0.00 to S.2.a.53. Occasional bursts of fire kept up with this trench.	
		10pm	Found enemy still firing all batteries turned on MARTINPUICH.	
	17	5am	Brigade turned on to German SWITCH trench from S.4.a.07 to M.33.a.61	
		9am	B/79 Shelled during morning. 2 guns put out of action. (Client A.C. WALKER. Suffering from Shell Shock.) Sergt Henry Wounded B/79	C.M.C.
	18		Sections fire all day.	
			All batteries registered new zone by one F.O.O in forward position M 36781 Sergt Abrey P. B/79 wounded	
			25174 Gnr Smith J. B/79	
	19		Same as yesterday. No 25647 Bob Thornton J. B/79 wounded	
	20	2.55am	Half Hour bombardment of British Trench Commenced	
		3.25	Infantry assaulted HIGH WOOD & attempted Barge & controlled road running from BAZENTIN-LE-PETIT to HIGH WOOD & LONGUEVAL	
		9am	Objectors reported to be gained and Infantry consolidating N. part of HIGH WOOD still held by enemy	
		10.30am	Enemy putting in heavy barrage between HIGH WOOD & the BAZENTINS, 3 heavily by gun 2nd line	C.M.C.
			Batteries reduced rate of fire to section fire 1 minute	
	21		Day and night firing carried on as usual	
	22	4.2pm	Major R. TURNBULL DR9 and 2Lt J.S. NEALE wounded	C.M.C.
		4.0pm	Enemy dell valley wounds of A C + D batteries very heavily for 5 minutes and repeated at 4.20pm, at 5.20pm and at 7.0pm	
		6.00	D/79 ordered to bombard trench south of N.W. corner of HIGH WOOD	
		7.0pm	General Bombardment of SWITCH TRENCH commenced and continues until 1.30am when Infantry assaulted Unsuccessful Barrage Established	C.M.C.

Army Form C. 2118

WAR DIARY
or
INTELLIGENCE SUMMARY

79th Bde R.F.A.   Page 19

(Erase heading not required.)

Place	Date July	Hour	Summary of Events and Information	Remarks and references to Appendices
FRICOURT	23		Fairly quiet day. The Brigade was relieved by the 256th Bde R.F.A. 51st Division (T)	C.M.C.
		10.30pm	Relief reported completed. Bde. ordered rendezvous at wagon lines & march to DERNANCOURT.	
DERNANCOURT	24		Brigade in camp, resting and refitting.	C.M.C.
	25		" "	
	26		" "	
	27		" "	
	28		" "	
	29		" "	
	30		" "	
	31		" "	

DWCurtis
Lieutenant Colonel
Commanding 79th Bde R.F.A.

79th Bde R.F.A.

Casualties &General during recent Operations:-

Killed. Officers. Nil.   Other ranks. 2.
Died of Wounds. Officers Nil   Other ranks. 2.
Wounded. Officers. Major P. Turnbull D/79   Other ranks. 19
                   2nd Lt. J.S. Neale B/79

Wastage from Sickness.
  Officers Major Hag Chanin B/79   Other ranks. 12.
  "   Lieut Sg Stewdard A/79

Casualties to Horses. Killed 1.   Wounded 1.

Ammunition Expended   18-pdr. Shrapnel   38,399
                              H.E.   16,710
                      4.5" How. H.E.   18,605

OW Lu Lu
79 Bde RFA
31/7
16

17th Divisional Artillery.

79th BRIGADE

ROYAL FIELD ARTILLERY.

AUGUST 1 9 1 6 ::

Ammunition expenditure.
Casualties.
Casualties animals.

WAR DIARY or INTELLIGENCE SUMMARY

79th Bde R.F.A.

Army Form C. 2118 Vol 13 Page 20

Place	Date August	Hour	Summary of Events and Information	Remarks and references to Appendices
DERNANCOURT	1	1.0 pm	Brigade marched to Fargue Hogan, leaving at MEAULTE, and thence proceeded into action, relieving and taking over from 166th Bde., 33rd Div. From 6.50 pm Heavy Howitzers bombarded from our wholepositions	CMC
		8.0 pm	Bde H.Q. established at S.20.a.5.4. Batteries in line, A, B, C, D from S.20.a.91 to S.11.c.64.	
Near BAZENTIN-LE-GRAND	2	5.30 pm	Bombardment of area old owe in rear carried out by all batteries	
			Casualties 2nd Lt Downing A/79 and No 72093 Gnr Reid H. B/79 Wounded	CMC
	3	2.40 am	Above Bombardment repeated	
		5.25	" " "	
		8.10 pm	" " " Batteries continued registration	
			Night firing continued. Bursts of fire in SWITCH TRENCH and in front	
		3.05.6 pm	Heavy Hostile Bombardment over whole position & neighbourhood at intervals.	CMC
		10 pm	Night firing on SWITCH TRENCH.	
	4		Casualties Killed No 20995 Gnr SORREL G.H. } A/79 No24359 Sergt COOK.A. No35078 Bdr WARE } B/79	
			114770 - BODIN W.M. A/79 12811 Gnr PARKER G.H } D/79	
			Wounded 2nd Lt. T. MARTIN A/79 Shell Shock.	
			No60142. Sergt JONES.E. No 70267 Gnr ATKINS J. No 20098 Gnr BLAND W. — A/79	
			11563 Gnr BROWN.W.M. No11650 Gnr HART.R — B/79	
			2488 Sergt. McGILL.J. 103551 Gnr STANHOPE.P.J. — D/79	
			ORCHARD TRENCH for 5 minutes by 18 pdrs 4.5 how 200 yards in rear	
	4	12.35 am	Intense Bombardment of ORCHARD TRENCH followed Infantry assaulted	CMC
		12.40	All guns lifted and published barrage on lines behind.	
		12.50	Barrage established on SWITCH TRENCH and kept up into daylight (4:30 am)	
		10.00 am	Was found infantry assault had not been successful. Batteries ordered Keep up shelling of ORCHARD TRENCH, ground in rear and TEA TRENCH	
			Casualties Wounded No 98650 Gnr BACON.H. H.Q. No 21162 Gnr JENKINSON A. C/79	
	5	9.0 pm	Barrage Bore (S.O.S.) Charged further to East Farm S.11.d.37 to S.12.a.2.1. N of DELVILLE WOOD	CMC
			Order for Day and Night firing to be carried on continuously on SWITCH TRENCH and area in rear	
			Allotment of Ammunition for Bde 18 pdr Day 500 Night 625, 4.5" How. Day 330 Night 166	
			Batteries registered new zone. Brigade on the whole Situation Generally fairly quiet. Hostile artillery less	
	6		active in medium range Enemy line by day and by night. Our Book area worked a communication	CMC
			trench. Firing was carried on by all batteries. Hostile Artillery fairly active in Bde Neighbourhood	
			Lieut J.D. DUTTON has joined 79th Bde, to command B/79 vice Major J.A.G. Charriol, evacuated to England sick on 25/7/16	
			No 4506 Gnr RAYENSCROFT D/79 Reported Missing	CMC

WAR DIARY or INTELLIGENCE SUMMARY

Army Form C. 2118

79th Bde R.F.A.   Page 21

Place	Date August	Hour	Summary of Events and Information	Remarks and references to Appendices
Near BAZENTIN -LE- GRAND	7	5.30 pm 6.20 " 11.40 " 12.0 " 9.	Bombardment of ORCHARD TRENCH, between DELVILLE WOOD and WOOD LANE lifted and Barrage established from S.11.d.9½ to S.11.d.08 ″ ″ ″ ″ ″ ″ ″ ″ S.11.d.9½ to S.12.16 by A, B, C, & D/B on usual programme. it ORCHARD TRENCH from S.11.d.57 to S.12.16 by A, B, C, & D/B on usual programme. Infantry attacked, A&C established Barrage 100 yds N. of Bde Barrage line. Hostile fire fairly heavy all round. Valley positioned during whole night. No casualties.	CWC
	8	7.40 am 10.30 am	Same programme as for 11.40 pm last night, followed by Infantry attack & Barrage from attack Line going field. D/79 ordered to put up slow barrage on ORCHARD TRENCH from S.11.d.08 to S.11.c.58. 20 rounds per hour. A, B, & C/79 to establish barrage line S.11.b.54 to S.11.a.43 including TEA TRENCH 30 minutes per B/y per hour.	CWC
		3.10 pm 3.20pm	D/79 ordered to Bombard N.edge of DELVILLE WOOD from S.12.c.06.k.27. 18pdrs Bombard S.11.a.59½ to S.12.c.19 Infantry attack on German Trench in W. DELVILLE WOOD, A, B-C barrage along TEA TRENCH S.11.6.6 to S.12.a.35″ Fairly quiet to Midnight. Batteries Registered on ORCHARD TRENCH S.11.b.64.7 - S.11.a.4.6.5 gun by gun.	
	9		Casualty. No. 98302 Gnr R. HOW. 4 C.N. wounded. Ordinary day and night firing carried on by all batteries.	
	10			
	11	10.30 pm	Sunday Barrage N.of Delville Wood raised. 60 rounds per Bde per hour. A, B, C Batteries put rather 2 hrs and the 6am Bay and Ry & being on usual. Opp bombarded and damaged MG emplacement "ORCHARD TRENCH." D/M Sunday Barrage N/DELVILLE WOOD started again and kept up with 5 am to cover Minor Operation of Infantry.	CWC
		7.30 pm	Casualties Wounded No.107968 Gnr HEWER C. A/79 No.36928 Gnr FROGGATT N.A. D/79	
	12		Quiet day. Usual day & night firing carried out. Hostile Battery positions at M12.a.27, 3.85 found by A.O.D/79	
	13		Usual day & night firing carried out. Hostile batteries reported active at S.6.b.81.86, S.6.d.77.9585, 98.6 500 ft. M.27.a.27 and M.28.d.88 were engaged several times during the day.	CWC
		9.30 pm	Heavy Barrage opened on Front line, & support trenches in Ration drawn by Bde. All intermediate kept firm at Barrage lane. Continued at Barrage rate for 10 minutes, then slowly down to Battery fire for 1 minute. Hostile fire slow & moderate, fairly casual it was reported but only little action. Same retaliation on tunnel S.11.a.H043 round the reserved. Enemy fatally much noting Barrage. Slight night firing returned.	
	14	10.30 pm	Casualties today No.40500 Gnr BAYERS.J all No.21147 Gnr HARRISON.H.V. wounded. Quiet morning, some shelling in vicinity of Bde. C.O. & B.C. of Bde 1/4 Barrain came up & Saw on Gun position previously taken over.	CWC

Army Form C. 2118

WAR DIARY
or
INTELLIGENCE SUMMARY

79th Bde RFA

Page 22

(Erase heading not required.)

Instructions regarding War Diaries and Intelligence Summaries are contained in F. S. Regs., Part II. and the Staff Manual respectively. Title Pages will be prepared in manuscript.

Place	Date August	Hour	Summary of Events and Information	Remarks and references to Appendices
Near BAZENTIN -LE- GRAND	15		Usual day and night firing carried out & Back Areas & some suspected battery positions shelled.	
	16		" " Registration of ORCHARD TRENCH TRENCH shelled fm nr OP in LONGUEVAL. Enfilade ORCHARD TRENCH. Gun moved in that night - position for forward gun just E. of BAZENTIN-LE-PETIT, to enfilade ORCHARD TRENCH.	
		5.0pm	Slow Bombardment started of ORCHARD TRENCH and back areas on Regt. of Infantry that enemy were preparing to attack. Barrage opened in our Front of TEA TRENCH afterwards lifted on to when been a lull fm gun in Bentradink area wound. Barrage stopped about 10.10 p.m.	CMcQ
		10.0pm	Night firing m Bentradink area wound. Casualties. M/93367 Cpl Bradley H. and M/98212 Dr McNulty J. Wounded 4/79	
	17	7am.	A/79 Registered New Enflade gun along ORCHARD TRENCH Slow continued bombardment of Brigade objectives continued Casualties. M 2119 Gnr BATTS. J, and M 6.2 Gnr DERRICK.C., No 113604 Gnr HICHOLS R. No B/79 Wounded.	CMcQ
	18	8.a.	Special Bombardment preparations on ORCHARD TRENCH Gombat back area commenced. Intense bombardment of ORCHARD TRENCH fm 8.40 to 8.47am and 12.10 to 12.19pm. } Hows in Infantry advanced. All 18pdrs lifted 5-200 yds beyond Infantry to creep out under cover of this } back area.	
		2.45p	Barrage established 400 yds N. of ORCHARD TRENCH while Infantry consolidated captured position. Barrage continued until dark.	
		2.50pm		
		3.0pm		
		3.20pm	Barrage lifted a further 200yds on request of Infantry. Hostile batt. scattering ground near (centre of 5.10pm)	
		9.0pm	1-18pdr put Battery pulled in new Barrage line about 200 yds beyond completed nor bombard. Remained in occasionally forced to Bazgrin - Men. Hows. some there. This is SOS Barrage for tonight all (except alone shi) kept on alr Barrage) gun in TEA TRENCH, TEA LANE & SUPPORT to assist	
		10.0pm	operations of S. Lanks. DELVILLE (w) 80D.	
		11.30pm	Heavy fire resumed and continued throughout night. Casualties during 24 hours previous (M 119019 Gnr BENNETT. J 14) B/79 Wd. McALLISTER. J. 2/4/79 Wounded. 1090 Bdr SCULL. J Gnr PARR. JM	CMcQ
	19	10.0am	All batteries put to establish Barrage, 120yards fm (they pr minute (1 tons 60 lb) 100 yds beyond S.O.S. line to prevent re-appearance of any of the nearby enemy in DELVILLE WOOD Rate of fire slacken Barrage when to 60 rds per hr 18 pdrs & 40 for Hows. Casualty. No 56206 Bdr DRAKE R. C/79 Wounded	CMcQ

WAR DIARY / INTELLIGENCE SUMMARY

79th Bde R.F.A.

Page 23

Army Form C. 2118

Place	Date August	Hour	Summary of Events and Information	Remarks and references to Appendices
Near BAZENTIN -LE- GRAND	20	10.0 am	Brigade Zone taken over for defensive purpose by 166th Bde R.F.A. Batteries ceased firing at this hour. Casualties previous 24 hours. No 21005 Sergt LISTER. L.W. C/79 N° 2340 Gnr THOMAS. W. B/79 Wounded. "97285" Gnr HUNT. J. " 118413 " HUDDERS. W "	CME
		3:30 pm	All Batteries guns now clear of Battery position.	
		5.0/-		
BONNAY	21.		Brigade marched to camp at BONNAY	
	22	8 am	Brigade Inspection and cleaning up. Inspected (with 17th Div. Art.) at 2:30 pm by Maj. Gen. HORNE. Commanding XV Corps	CME
			Brigade March to CARDONETTE and horses. Arrived 11.15 am	
CARDONETTE	23	1.45pm	" - OCCOCHES. Arrived 9.30 p.m.	
OCCOCHES	24	6.0 am	" - GAUDIEMPRE " 11.30 a.m.	
GAUDIEMPRE	25		Resting, cleaning up &c. C.O. & B.C's to meet CRA. at 17 D.A. IHQ at 9.30 a.m. to reconnoitre	CME
	26		All guns to I.O.M. FREVENT for overhaul.	
	27			
	28	8 pm	One section of each Battery 79th Bde. relieved a section of each Battery 282nd Bde. (Northern Group)	
	29		in action	
	30			
	31	9 pm	Remaining sections of Batteries relieved sections of Southern Group batteries. 3 sections of 80th Bde. joined A, B & C batteries at larger dumps preparatory to engaging Batteries now in action as 48th Batteries. Group Consists of 8 Batteries & lightning	CME
			Position - A/79 at K.8 d. 1500 map sheet. 57.D.	
			B/79 " K.13 a. 87 95	
			C/79 " K.13 a. 2030	
			D/79 " K.15 d. 4085	
			C/80 " K.8 a. 6050	

D.W. Curtis
Lieut-Colonel
Comd. 2 79th Bde. R.F.A.

79th Bde R.F.A.

Ammunition Expended during Month of August. 1916.
A. 22,792.   Ax 7901.   Bx 9754.

Casualties during Month of August 1916.
Killed   Officers. Nil.   O.R. 6.
Died of Wounds   "   Nil   O.R. 3
Wounded   "   1   O.R. 29.
Missing   "   Nil   O.R. 1.

Casualties to Horses Killed 5.   Wounded 12.

Wastage from Sickness during month of August.
Officers 1.   O.R. 10

WAR DIARY or INTELLIGENCE SUMMARY

Army Form C. 2118

79th Bde R.F.A.

Vol 14 page 29

Place	Date Sept.	Hour	Summary of Events and Information	Remarks and references to Appendices
SAILLY - AU - BOIS	1	10.a.m.	Command of Southern Group passed to O.C. 79th Bde R.F.A. Batteries engaged checking registration lines &c. and completing reorganization. 79th Bde was reorganized as a Brigade of Three six-gun 18 pdr Batteries, one 4.5" How. Bty. By absorption of B/50 sections from B and C/50 R.H.A. as follows A/79 plus 1 section B/50 under command of Capt HCR Gross. B/79 " " " " - Capt H.F. Nottage C/79 " " C/50 " " - Capt CMR Take D/79 as before - Capt E. Nottidge.	CMC
	2			
	3			
	4		Hours tested surface. Working parties sheet many areas occasionally exposed by enemy.	CMC
		8.30pm & 11.30pm	In conjunction with discharge of gas by 2nd Divsn. (mainly a borbardmt. of flanks of Black sector) was carried out by A, C & D batteries — 670 rounds A, 30 rounds A x B 255 rounds B x	
	5		Quiet day.	
	6	8.30pm	Gas discharge in front of Brigade on our left. This divn. in conjunction with neighbours of GOMMECOURT was bombarded by A, B & C batteries — 280 rds A. 150 A x little activity in Group front. Holcus participated in. Third sect B/79 moved to posn 200x in front of remainder of Batty, at K.16 a.52. Sect A/79 moved to K.14 d.52. This is part of Centre Group's inflated trench MHp Gommicourt Salient.	CMC
	7		Quiet day. Little activity.	
	8			
	9	6.30pm	Short bombardment of GOMMIECOURT in conjunction with Centre Group. 140 A x 45 B x	
	10	8.00pm	C + D batteries opened fire 20 rounds each on Trunk Matter trench about K.17.b.29.	
		1.15pm	All batteries fired at a combined shoot at "FARMYARD" neighbourhood to report of enemy infantry who were being arranged by Trunk Matter in this area. Casualty 179902 Gnr BURNSIDE W. C/79 Wounded.	CMC
	11		P.S. Following men in a.ed. getting men & ammunition & building trenches of exposures &c. Werrall Kelly Gale, Winchmore Luton, Casualty 10895 Sgt J. Sullivan C/9 Wounded.	CMC
	12			CMC

WAR DIARY or INTELLIGENCE SUMMARY

Army Form C. 2118

79th Bde R.F.A. Page 25

Place	Date	Hour	Summary of Events and Information	Remarks and references to Appendices
SAILLY AU BOIS	13	7.0pm	Retaliation for shelly for half hr, caused by 4 batteries at request of Infantry.	
	14		B battery continued Barbed wire gap in wire strafe on 11's 200 yds front	
	15		A. B. Batteries wire cutting. 3 gaps left open at night by request of Infantry	
	16		do do do do 200 yds.	CMC
	17		Wire cutting suspended. Wind took leaflets in our face	
	18			
	19	12 m.n.	One section of each battery relieved by 166th Bde R.F.A. and one section each 18pdr battery withdrawn from line in addition	
	20	6 p.m.	Remaining section of 4 batteries relieved. Command of Southern Group passed to 166th Bde	CMC
PAS.	21	7.50 am	79th Bde at PAS Huts. Brigade marched to BEALCOURT and billetted for night	
BEALCOURT	22	12 noon	" " Nest-Crew at VITZ-VILLEROY	
VILLEROY	23		Training commenced under Brigade arrangements	
	24		" continued	
	25		" "	
	26		" "	
	27		" "	
	28	11.30pm	Brigade received orders to be ready to move at 1 hour's notice	
	29	12.15pm	Brigade marched to MEZEROLLES and billetted for night	
	30	12.50pm	" " PAS HUTS. Working Parties were sent forward at 7am by motor	CMC
			lorry to start work on new gun position near HEBUTERNE	

CM Cavell
Lt & adjt.
for Lieut Colonel
Comdg 79th Bde R.F.A.

79th Bde R.F.A.

Ammunition expended during the month of September 1916
A 4129   Ax 1697   B 4   Bx 558   Bps 33

Casualties during month of September
Killed   Officers   nil   O.R.   nil
Wounded   nil   O.R.   3

Casualties to Horses
nil.

Wastage from Section during month of August.
Officers nil   O.R.   48

G.J. Caird
A/Capt.
for Lt Col.
Comd. 79 Bde R.F.A.

WAR DIARY or INTELLIGENCE SUMMARY

Army Form C. 2118

79 Bde RFA Vol 15

Place	Date OCT.	Hour	Summary of Events and Information	Remarks and references to Appendices
PAS HUTS	1st		25 men per 18 pr battery under an officer from each battery continued work on new gun positions near HEBUTERNE. Bivouac netting at PAS HUTS.	W.B.J.
	2nd		Work continued, assisted by working party of 35 men from D.A.C.	
	3rd		Work continued. Communication with O.P's established.	
HEBUTERNE		6 pm to 9 pm	A.13. & C batteries (less 2 guns at Heavy Mobile Workshops) took up positions at K.15.a. 33.07. One Section of Howitzer Bty took over position at K.14.b. 80.30. and K.15.c. 45.30. respectively. One gun from Howr sent to J.18.b.1.8.	W.B.J.
	4th	8 am	at K.15.d. 50.95. from D/230 Bde FATE, BARNYARD, FAIR, FACE	
		10 am	Registration of enemy's wire in front of FATE, BARNYARD, FAIR, FACE begun. " " " " 300 prs shrapnel fires per gun	
		8 pm	Small gaps cut in front of each. Wire trenches & considerable amount damaged.	
			Remaining Section of D/79 (How) went into action at K.15.d. 50.95.	
	5th	8 am	Wirecutting continued, in front of FALL, FARM, FAT. D/79 registered on front line wire	Vol.7
		10 am	79th Bde took over the line for defensive purposes from 230 Bde. 3 guns from K.17.b.1.8.(SUNKEN RD) to K.10.b.9.9. Howrs 79 Bde moved into Howr. allowance 500 RA per gun.	
SAILLY AU BOIS	6th	8 am	Wirecutting resumed (1 in front) FACE, FAIR, FARM, YARD. Ammunition unlimited. 17 guns in action (1 bt 3rd Army Workshops) 50 RSA 10 AX to Hows.	Vol.7
	7th	8 am	Wirecutting continued at same points as yesterday. Amm. allowance extremely difficult per gun	
	8th	8 am to 12.3 pt	Wirecutting in front of FACT, FABLE & FANCY. Observation difficult Non visibility prevent shower of rain	W.B.J.
	9th	10 am to 4 pm	Wirecutting in front of "FANCY and "FAT. Observation difficult	
	10	10.6 5 pm	Wirecutting " FANCY, FAT, FALL. One gun from 3 18 pr Batteries detached to form a composite battery at K.13.C.40.6.0. Composite Bty registered	
	10-11	8 pm to 6 am	Composite 6 bts fires in the gaps in enemy and to stop working parties repairing same.	W.B.J.
	11"	10 am	Wirecutting continued. Composite Bty fires 60 rds AX at regular intervals	
	12"	10 pm	" During each night

WAR DIARY or INTELLIGENCE SUMMARY

Army Form C. 2118

Place	Date Oct.	Hour	Summary of Events and Information	Remarks and references to Appendices
HEBUTERNE	13th	9.0 am	The 3. 18 Pr. Batteries of the 79 Bde took places at the disposal of the 33rd Division for purpose of wire cutting. In defence of the line they remained under the orders of R.17th Div. Art.	AAA ?
	14th	7.30	Wire cutting continued on FAIR, FACE, FARMYARD & FARMER. 258 Rds Shrapnel	
	15th	8.30	Wire cutting continued. 330 Rds Shrapnel per 18 pr. per battery allowed.	AAA ?
	16th		Wire cutting continued. 100 Rds H.E. per gun each night at irregular intervals.	
		6.30 pm	Though Enemy maintained his usual Battery positions	
		6.30 pm	2 Sections from each Battery withdrawn to Wagon lines & 1 Section of Howitzers	
PAS HUTS	17th		Remaining Sections withdrawn to Wagon Lines with Hqrs.	
	18th	10.30 am	79 Bde marched to ALBERT with Wagon lines at W.28.a.9.6. Reconnaissance for Battery Commander.	AAA ?
ALBERT	19th	6.30 am	Reconnaissance for Battery positions by Battery Commanders.	
	20th	6.0 am	Rigging parties at work digging new battery positions near forward positions	
			Batteries in Echelon A/79 at R.33.a.60.85. B/79 R.27.c.4.0. C/79 R.27.c.4.2.	
			D/79 at R.23.a.7.0. Bde Hqrs. at R.32.d.1.2. B.S.S.G. STRUDWICK wounded.	AAA ?
			Great difficulty experienced in carting RE materials to gun positions, also ammunition, owing to Mud, bad state of road and roads that not weather.	
	21st		Digging continued. One Section French Bty with full echelon met into action.	
	22nd	3 pm	Capt. H.J. Cannon wounded. Remaining guns went into action with full echelon.	
	23rd	9 am	79th Bde took over defence of the line with 19th Brigade R.F.A. Guns with Forward Section Observation from REGINA TRENCH.	AAA ?
			& covering the 57th Inf Bde 19th Brigade Hqrs established at R.32.d.1.2.	
		10 am	2 Batteries registered.	
	24th	3 pm	Remaining batteries registered.	
		9 am	Wire cutting began. Flights of rain on target. Whilst vehicle weather	AAA ?
			Pack-horses and mules used for supply of ammunition	

WAR DIARY
or
INTELLIGENCE SUMMARY

(Erase heading not required.)

Army Form C. 2118

Instructions regarding War Diaries and Intelligence Summaries are contained in F. S. Regs., Part II. and the Staff Manual respectively. Title Pages will be prepared in manuscript.

Place	Date Oct	Hour	Summary of Events and Information	Remarks and references to Appendices
	25th	8 am	Wire cutting in GRANDCOURT TRENCH continued. Parties of enemy seen and dispersed. Wounded 1 O.R. Gnr SAUNDERS W. (1°95117) Shell pc.	W.W.D.
	26th	6/7pm 5.15/6am 8 am	Night firing on enemy's intercommunication from 6pm to 6am. Barrage established maintained in front of Sugar Trench, Rifle Regina & Infantry on left who sent up S.O.S. Wire cutting continued. fire kept up and dispersed. Wounded in forehead. 1 O.R. No 11668 Gnr MOLES W. (Shell pc.) Defences fired on by Stokes gun. Wounded 1 O.R. No 11668 Gnr MOLES W. (Shell pc.) Night firing on enemy at usual	W.W.D. —
	27th		Night firing as usual. Wire cutting continued. Several new targets registered.	W.W.D.
	28th	2.0 pm	Wire cutting continued. Parties of enemy fired on & dispersed. Hostile battery in action located at L.33.c.4.5. engaged by 4/79 Several direct hits observed. Battery ceased fire after first/last/direct hit. Germans found alive in dugout in REGINA TRENCH when they had been buried since capture of trench by British on Oct 21st	W.W.D.
	29th	6.0 am	Wire cutting continued. Enemy in defence works Brownism very difficult. Horse wounds by shell. Barrage S.O.S. believing his status sustains very effective. Night firing as usual. Wounded No 92684 Gnr STILLWELL A. No 114558 Gnr BADGER H.	W.W.D.
	30	8.0am	Wire cutting continued. Visibility low. Wounded by shell.	
		11.30pm	Infantry patrols reports to F.O.O. that enemy working party was busy on new trench R. 15.d S.S.	W.W.D.
	31.	12.30 am to 12.55pm 8.0am 11.0am	Intensive bombardment for 5 minutes on enemy's front line infantry support. Wire cutting Hostile battery firing at L.33.c.45. shell Bty again reported active at Howitzer B.5. Shell Bty again reported active at 2.30 previously engaged. Wounded by shell 4 2 Gr. 20092 Gnr WALLER W. Lieut E.R. CURTICE Wounded by shell & 39665 Dr SUNDERLAND W. to W.20.L. (ALBERT Sheet) began own moved to W.20.L. (ALBERT Sheet) Lt. Col. Comdg. 79 Z. F. a. B. M.W. Castle	W.W.D.

1875 Wt. W593/826 1,000,000 4/15 J.B.C. & A. A.D.S.S./Forms/C. 2118.

79th Bde. R.F.A.

Ammunition expended during the month of October 1916.

A. 22,118. AX. 8851. B. 29. BX. 1140. BPS. 19.

Casualties during month of ~~September~~ October.
Killed   Officers Nil   O.R. 1
Wounded   "   3   O.R. 14

Casualties to Horses. Killed 5 Wounded (G.S.W.) 5.
Evacuated to Mobile Vet. Sect. 8.
O.R. 14

Wastage from sickness during month of October.
Officers Nil

NW Marsh
Lt Col.
Comdg 79 F.A.B.

WAR DIARY or INTELLIGENCE SUMMARY

Army Form C. 2118

Vol 16
1915. LAH Bde

Place	Date November	Hour	Summary of Events and Information	Remarks and references to Appendices
ALBERT	1st	2 am	Wounded soldier in billet at ALBERT. 1. O.R. No 21114. Gnr Handley W. (G.S.W.) } A/79 Killed 1 O.R. No 135224. Gnr Dunkley R. (G.S.W.)	
			Batteries in action as follows: A/79 at R.33.a.60.85. B/79 at R.27.c.40.70 Kagan Line at W.20.b. De MOUQUET FARM. C/79 at R.27.C.40.20 D/79 at R.33.a.70.00 HQrs at R.32.d.10.20	toB?
		6.30 am	Wire cutting in front of GRANDCOURT TRENCH.	
		3.20 pm	Shelling enemy infantry retiring at L.33.d.5.6 C/79 immediate (wounded) No 37298 Gnr KITCHEN G.	
		6.17 pm	Intermittent fire throughout the night, kept up on enemy defences.	
		9.0 am	Brigade Commander visited Bryne S.O.S Baryt., Vauxhall. very low	
	2nd		Enemy guns fired on also Battery position at L.33.C.4.5	WP?
		6 pm	Night firing as usual	
	3rd	9 am to 4 pm	Enemy wire + defences looks fired on also 30 Rds late at Hostile B7 reports Actual by R.F.C. at L.33.d.4.6.	
		6 pm	Night firing as usual. Casualties (by shrapnel) 1 O.R. (wounded) No 25447 A/Bdr SUTHERLAND R.A. A/79 No 96603 a/Bdr. JAMES F. C/79	k/d?
	4th	11 am	Hostile battery engaged and silenced at R.9.a.80.85. Ammunition pit blown up by D/79.	
		3.45 pm	Aeroplane registration of new trench point. R.16.a.5.3. also registration by F.O.O of our works at R.3.c.6.2	
			Orders received to reduce amount of ammunition at guns from 650 to 450 Rds per gun.	k/d?
		6 pm	Night firing as usual. Night quiet	
	5th	9 am	Intermittent fire throughout day on enemy defences; Howitzers fired on B5 position at L.33.c.4.5. 60 Rds HE also fired on B5 position at R.4.a.0.6.	
		8 pm	Enemy evening party digging at R.3.c.6.2. Casualties: (wounded) No 2459 Bdr MASON W. No 118473 Gnr HUDDERS W. (G.S.W.)	k/d?

Army Form C. 2118

WAR DIARY
or
INTELLIGENCE SUMMARY
(Erase heading not required.)

Instructions regarding War Diaries and Intelligence Summaries are contained in F. S. Regs., Part II. and the Staff Manual respectively. Title Pages will be prepared in manuscript.

Place	Date Nov.	Hour	Summary of Events and Information	Remarks and references to Appendices
ALBERT. positions at MOUQUET FARM	6.	9 a.m.	One irregular Shrapnel fire kept up throughout on Bridge over the R. ANCRE at R.4.d.1.5 and R.4.c.7.7. Howitzers fired 150 Rds B.X. on dugouts in banks at R.9.b.70.30 & R.9.c.95.35. Guns registered to keep enemy's dumps at important pts up to 6500 Rds. per gun. F.O.O. reports GRANDCOURT TRENCH so much damaged that enemy is visible & abnormal. Passing dugouts in parapet. Parties of enemy fired on & dispersed.	WD 2
	7.	6 pm	Howitzer firing on wood in Bridges, trenches, huts & approaches	
		9 a.m.	Firing on same targets as yesterday. 150 Rds on Bridge. Hows fired on B5, R.10.A.O.7. and B5, fired 30 Rds HE in retaliation on GRANDCOURT TRENCH at enemy's request	WD 3
		3 pm	Enemy retaliates on B5 positions with 105 mm shell. No casualties	
	8.	6 pm	Howitzer firing as usual. D.A. "No more ammn" Fire cut down to B5 positions	
		9 pm	Gdns receives from Battery	
		9 a.m.	Usual tasks by Batteries	
		11 am	F.O.O. reports REGINA & HESSIAN TRENCHES heavily shelled.	
			Capt. C.B. Group called on; retaliation proves effective.	
			Hostile aeroplane unusually active all day. Our A.A. fire ineffective.	
		4.30 pm	Enemy fired about 5 Rds 4.2 in. shells into D/79 position.	
			One direct hit on dugout killed instantly 2 Gunners CAPT EDWARD NOTTIDGE and LIEUT JAMES SUTHERLAND BRIMMS 2nd in command, 2nd in command and No 60703 Bdr COCKMAN C.F.	WD 2
	9.	6 pm	Slight firing carried out as before.	
		9 am	Enemy's bad temperance fired on & trenches enfiladed. Howitzers fired on dugouts in R.15.b.	
	10.	6 pm	Slight firing to as before	
		10.30 pm	Enemy shells Battery position with gas shell, intermittent until midnight.	
		5.30 am	Intense bombardment of DESIRE & GRANDCOURT TRENCHES with H.E. 6-9 am.	
		7 a.m.	Guns in action firing many rounds. Hostile fire very active. Dugouts in parapet Several until 12.15. Much matériel Comrades bringing through enemy telephone traffic down at noon by R.A. fire	

WAR DIARY
or
INTELLIGENCE SUMMARY

(Erase heading not required.)

Army Form C. 2118

Instructions regarding War Diaries and Intelligence Summaries are contained in F. S. Regs., Part II and the Staff Manual respectively. Title Pages will be prepared in manuscript.

Place	Date NOV.	Hour	Summary of Events and Information	Remarks and references to Appendices
	11th	6.30 pm	Wounded 1 O.R. No 28891 SERGT CASEY J. (Effects of gas on night 9-10th inst.)	
	16.	5.30.	Bombardment of DESIRE & GRANDCOURT TRENCHES. Intercommunication trench at Intervals dealt with about 80 4.2" shells. Full enemy bde H.Qrs.	W.0.2
		6.0 am	Enemy's trenches & shell holes in front & rear searched by 18 pdrs.	
		7. am to am	Enemy's bombard enemy's strong points & dugouts situated GRANDCOURT TRENCH at R.16.a.8.7.	
		7 am	Fire on party by A/79 & dispersed.	
		9 am	Fog renders observation impossible. Same condition for remainder of day.	
		6. pm	Night firing as usual.	
	12.	5.30 am	Bombardment on shelters until 6. AM. Very little retaliation on batteries or trenches.	
		7. PM	Deliberate bombardment of dugouts & enemy defences by Stokes Mortars also 18 pdrs. Position at 2.33.e.4.8. Stokes Mortars brought fire kept up by 18 pdrs on A/79 mortars. BEAUREGARD DOVECOTE	W.0.2
		3.50 pm	and VICINITY heavily shelled all day. Ammun. expended 500 Rds 18 pdr 240 Rds How. Enemy trenches	
	13.		Casualty wounded (gas poisoning) 1. O.R. Gnr HUNT A.E. (97 pdrs)	
	13.	5.45 am	Attack began of the whole German Front line by V & II Corps astride by from appx. K. 17 To R. 21 a.O.8, Barrage on GRANDCOURT TRENCH & Beaucourt. Full concentration by 18 pdrs on ground between REGINA & GRANDCOURT TRENCH at vaumetre & 4. (PHASE I 9. 17. D.A. OID. 59 consulted)	
		8.4 hr	No infantry assault on our Brigade front.	
		6.0 hr	Between our left bgde front & R. ANCRE. the 19th Div. & 39 Div Captured the Machine in HANSA LINE between R. ANCRE & RAILWAY ROAD near River ANCRE.	
		6.13 am	From 6.13 am slow protective barrage by (D/79 & B/79) on GRANDCOURT Trench.	
		7. am	Batteries ceased fire.	
		9.0 am	Bty from morning until normal expenditure. Battery fire on enemy defences. A/79 3 O.R. N° 72069 B: FEATHERSTONE J Sanitation 20596 G. COOPER J. R. 11.2183 G. JAMES F. J. 20970 G. COOK L.W.	
			Admitted to Hospital. 2/Lt. R. H. SANDON. (D/79) C/79 1 OR.	

WAR DIARY
or
INTELLIGENCE SUMMARY

(Erase heading not required.)

Army Form C. 2118

Place	Date NOV.	Hour	Summary of Events and Information	Remarks and references to Appendices
	14th	7.30 AM	Enemy confined to GRANDCOURT TRENCH after intense bombardment from 6.0 to 6.30. Slow rate of fire maintained. Round 1/HE, bursting on Chamber & Jam of A/79. Barrage the piece. Gun withdrawn from position.	
		12.30pm	Infantry flight refuses to aeroplane. 70 RO Shrapnel fired on R.B.C. Guns remark. Aeroplane reports hostile battery active at R.4.b.50.70. Barrage put 30 Rds BX into position.	W.T.2
		3 pm	NGV firing on road from 1 A/79 continuous for scoring. 6 approaches with evidence tonight.	
	15th	6 pm		
		4 pm		
		7 am	Open history of A/79 continuous for scoring & roads down from position.	
		1 pm	Registration of Shrapnel Barrage on enemy's trenches throughout the day.	
		5.15 pm	Reported S.O.S. on our left. Barrage maintained a slow barrage on S.O.S. for 15 mins until ling Casualties. Bar. (A.S.W.) 88489 Gr. Nixon. P. 113121 Gr. Buck W.H. 18/79 26521 Gr. Denman T.	NOEL 8/79
	16th		Day might firing as usual. 3 hostile spherical balloons were sent over by the enemy, two were seen in neighborhood of POZIERES	MW
	16.	2.30 pm		
	17th		Day & night firing as usual.	
	17th	6.15 am	Two Landsman A/N A/79 Captured an armed private of the 173rd Regt in a shell hole near HESSIAN TRENCH and handed him to the Right Batt. (10 Buffs 55th Infy Bde)	IRW.
		7 am	A convoy of motor lorries at R.9.b was of superior hostile aeroplane was fired on by C/79	MW.

Army Form C. 2118

WAR DIARY
or
INTELLIGENCE SUMMARY
(Erase heading not required.)

Place	Date Nov.	Hour	Summary of Events and Information	Remarks and references to Appendices
	18th	6 AM	"Zero hour". Intense bombardment of DESIRE TRENCH. Infantry assault GRANDCOURT DESIRE TRENCH	
		6.24	Objective taken on our front, + on Heights. Brigade on the left held up.	
		6.30 am	Barrage on GRANDCOURT TRENCH. Rate of fire slowed down.	
		11.30	Rate of fire on GRANDCOURT TRENCH slowed down to 30 rds per bty per hour	
		2.24 pm	" " " " " 20 R.P " " "	WD
		5.50 pm	S.O.S. Barrage on GRANDCOURT TRENCH. Hostguns in action from GRANDCOURT VILLAGE. No retaliation on Batteries.	
			Night firing on Nos targets throughout night. Wounded 1 O.R. No 22922 Gnr. MAIR T. Div. MAIR T. Nov. 21st	WD
	19th	12.5 pm	Orders received that Brigade will 17th Div Art. will join Fourth Army in GRANDCOURT TRENCH.	
		4.30 pm	Stern reports that enemy were moving in GRANDCOURT TRENCH.	
			A/79 + C/79 each fired 30 rds for 2 mins on CROSS TRENCH a French	
			B/79 fired 30 rds on CROSS TRENCH reports though held by enemy trackers.	WD
		6 hrs	Batt rounds fired every night at irregular intervals on used targets.	
	20th	7 am	17th Div. Art. takes over the defence of the line to 11th + 19th Div. Art.	
		8 am	A/79 moved from position near MOUQUET FARM.	
			B/79 "	
		9 am	C/79 "	
		11 am	H.Q.79 moves to Wagon Lines.	
		3 pm	Guns received trucked to MEAULTE 10.30am on 21st	
			Bde marches to new Wagon Lines E. 29 a. S.W. of MEAULTE.	
	21st	10 am	Brigade cleaning up & refitting.	WD

Army Form C. 2118

WAR DIARY
or
INTELLIGENCE SUMMARY
(Erase heading not required.)

Instructions regarding War Diaries and Intelligence Summaries are contained in F. S. Regs., Part II. and the Staff Manual respectively. Title Pages will be prepared in manuscript.

Place	Date Nov	Hour	Summary of Events and Information	Remarks and references to Appendices
MEAULTE	22nd		Brigade resting & refitting. Leave quota 6 "leaves" per day allotted to Bde.	WW
	23rd		A/79 drew 1 new gun carriage & 1 new piece from Ordnance.	
	24th		Overhauling of guns begun at horse lines. do.	
	25th		do. do.	MW
	26th		Batteries moved into wagon lines A.B.C/79 to A.B.C/79 to E 27d. E/79 to E 28 central. Brigade moved to E 27 d & 6.2 Brigade relieved the Brigade. Command assumed 9p 8/79.	MW
	27th		Brigade resting and refitting.	MW
	28th		do. do.	MW
	29th		do. do.	MW
	30th		do. do.	MW

79th Bde. R.F.A.

Ammunition Expended during the month of November 1916

15604 A   7720 AX   56 B.   4078 BX

Casualties during the month of November 1916

Killed   Officers 2   O.R. 2
Wounded   "   Nil   "   16
                               ——
                               18

Casualties Horses Killed 4. Evacuated to Mobile Vety Section 33
                              Destroyed 2 Lost 2

Wastage from Sickness — Officers Nil   O.R. 20.

[signature]
Major Comdg. 79th FAB

WAR DIARY
or
INTELLIGENCE SUMMARY

(Erase heading not required.)

Army Form C. 2118

Vol 17
4th A Bde Ac

Place	Date 1916	Hour	Summary of Events and Information	Remarks and references to Appendices
MEAULTE	Dec 1		Brigade resting refitting.	
	2		" " "	
	3		" " "	
	4		" " "	App?
	5		" " "	
	6		" " "	
	7		" " "	
	8		" " "	
	9	9 am	3 Officers & 6 NCOs per Battery proceeded to Battery position occupied by 78th FAB. to take over	App?
			positions front OPs etc.	
	10	8 am	Advance parties from each battery & Bde proceeded to new positions	App?
			Detachments spend the night at Bryon huts CARNOY	
	11	8 am	Brigade moved from huts to CARNOY	
		2 pm	79th Bde RFA over the defense of the line from 78th FAB	
			Hqrs at T.20.a.5.4. (2 Horse arty in action)	
			A/79 at T.9.d.3.2.	
			B/79 " T.9.c.7.7.	
			D/79 " T.9.d.2.1.	
			Bde 3rm from N.36.d.4.2. to T.5.b.80.95.	
			all guns from 78th Bde were taken over complete in position + 79th guns handed	
			over to Louis.	
		6 pm	Relief complete	App?
			Night fairy an enemy broken trench.	

WAR DIARY
or
INTELLIGENCE SUMMARY

Army Form C. 2118

Place	Date	Hour	Summary of Events and Information	Remarks and references to Appendices
GINCHY (hut)	12	9 am	Burst of fire throughout day on enemy trenches + back areas.	WD
		5 pm	B/79 reported HE bursting one hundred yds front our action with damage twice. Bde arms allotment - fires at 4.20. A×. ser. B× 209. Night gun cruise at on C.To rotch between front line + main BAPAUME ROAD.	
	13	9 am	Re registration on gun lines + other targets. Wind dry from NEW position for D/79 reconnoitred and chosen at T.16.a.2.6. B/79 had a second gun put out of action this' premature in gun. Night fires in trenches + roads in Bn. Zone.	WD
	14	7 am	Batteries 2 ranged guns from positions. Heavy hostile shelling throughout this zone. Battery 7.3 am replies. For 13 minutes to B'dge 7.5 pm. reports all quiet. D/79 coming in new position enters and J TRANSLOY + trench x roads.	WD
	15	7 am	+ 7 TRANSLOY (9.7°A Bde) tough - intercharge by D/79 at new position to from 1-2 g/79 withdrew from covered perken to back position. 3 gun registration on zero lines. Light gun + trench lines.	WD
	16	8 am	A/79 Wire cutting. Reconnaissance for 2 forward guns B/79 at S T.18 a.0090. Wire dry trough + from covers cut.	WD

Army Form C. 2118

WAR DIARY
or
INTELLIGENCE SUMMARY
(Erase heading not required.)

Instructions regarding War Diaries and Intelligence Summaries are contained in F. S. Regs., Part II and the Staff Manual respectively. Title Pages will be prepared in manuscript.

Place	Date	Hour	Summary of Events and Information	Remarks and references to Appendices
XIX	17	8 AM	2 Guns trying to fire to 13/79 position. Fire then at E.O.M. Bursts few. Hostyled gas an TREACLE TRENCH.	WD
		6 pm	No incidents - very few hostile. 2 guns 13/79 in return opened MOIN TRENCH	
	18th	9 am to 3 pm	Night quiet. 13/79 registered 2 germ guns. 4 Howitzers at new positions on Bowler's front line. 200 Rds. A defended in wire cutting.	WD
		4 to 6 pm	Enemy trenches bombarded with shrapnel. 7/HE. 1/8pt working on OP 7.10 + T 2.5. trimming parties observed. No construction of any import. Heavy night firing	WD
	19th	9 am	13/79 continued wire cutting. 13/79 fired HE. on enemy defences. A/79 continued on trenches + OP.	WD
	20th	9 am	Heavy style firing. M/79 fired on trenches at Serre ; - observed a party of enemy at BAPAUME Rd, fired on. Casualties 1 OR. No 13982. Dr DAVIES R.G. (GSW) wounded.	WD
	21st	9 am to 3.30 pm	Night firing on kite balloon. Gap from wire cutting	WD
	22"	—	As yesterday	WD
	23rd	—	No. 1 Howitzer out of action with damages trail shackles of recoil	WD

WAR DIARY or INTELLIGENCE SUMMARY

Army Form C. 2118

Place	Date	Hour	Summary of Events and Information	Remarks and references to Appendices
	24th	9 am	Day firing on all ground near enemy defences S.E. of LE TRANSLOY. Stamps Howitzers replied.	W62
		10 pm	All T.M. men attached to 79" Bde returns to Harincourt.	
		12.3. to 6 pm	Night firing as usual on tracks & trenches.	
	25th	8.30 am to 8.45	Bombardment - Enemy front line by Right Group. (Left-Arty Operation Order No 7). (10 minutes intense) fire	W63
		10 pm	C.R.A. 17th Divl Arty. assumes command of Left Arty. XIV Corps. C.R.A. 2nd Divl Arty relieved. O.C. 79" FAB assumes command of Right Arty Group.	
		11.30	15 minutes intense bombardment. Enemy strong point by Right Group, also by all Arty on Corps front. Our fire reported by Reports with Wiltshire.	
		5 pm	Night firing very effective.	
	26th	9 am	Registration of points in enemy front line and C.T.'s	W67
		12 Noon to 4 pm	Bombardment. Enemy front line, C.T.'s & strong points by XIV Corps Artillery (Left Arthy Operation Order No 6) Intense fire (except for 2 short bursts) throughout. (Infantry fire) was shelln— No infantry assault. Casualty Lce Corpl ARNEY C. 6/79 killed (E.S.W.)	W67
	27th 28th	9 am	Night firing on Sunken Roads & tracks in Bée 3rd night firing on tracks sunken roads & night firing crossroads.	W67
		"	"	
		"	"	

Army Form C. 2118

WAR DIARY
or
INTELLIGENCE SUMMARY
(Erase heading not required.)

Place	Date	Hour	Summary of Events and Information	Remarks and references to Appendices
GINCHY	29th	9 pm to 4 pm	Usual day firing on enemy trenches, tracks & defences. Working parts observed + fired on (dispersed). Registration of strong points & trench junctions on front line.	W.D.
		4.30 pm	Night firing in undisturbed tracks roads	
	30th	2 pm	Lift Artillery XIV Corps O.O. No 8. Counter-Bombardment of enemy trenches for 30 minutes in zone N.36.b. & 31.c. & U.1.a.	W.D.
		3 pm	Wire cut in multiple & enemy trenches MORVAL + LESBŒUFS. Honeycomb trench lightly scratched & reported between 3 am & 9 pm in zone N.36.b.c.t.d. & 31 a. + c. as it is believed	
		9 pm	a Relief taking place in that sector.	
	31.	12.5 am	2/17 Bde called for S.O.S. Barrage + Enemy received report that S.O.J. Broken later Enemy put up an air light panel. Barrage established transferred for 4 minutes when F.O.O. reports all quiet. Batteries returned to normal night firing	W.D.
		9 am to 4 pm	Day firing as usual. 18 prs on trenches, Howitzers on dugouts & gun pits in back zone.	

N W Cushies
Lieut Col comdg 79 Bde R.F.A.

79th Brigade R.F.A.

1. Ammunition expended during the month of December
   "A" 3140 Rds. "AX" 12,389. "BX" 4,516.

2. Casualties during the month of December.
   Killed.   Officers – Nil.   O.R. 1.
   Wounded. Officers – Nil.   O.R. 2.

3. Casualties to Horses. – Killed NIL.
   Destroyed } 20.
   or died   }
   Evacuated to Mobile Vet. Section – 32.
   Missing 1.

4. Knotage from sickness.
   Officers 1.
   O.R.   41.

   N.W. ....
   Lieut. Col. Cmdg. 79th Bde R.F.A.

Army Form C. 2118.

WAR DIARY
or
INTELLIGENCE SUMMARY
(Erase heading not required.)

79th Brigade R.F.A. 17th Division

Instructions regarding War Diaries and Intelligence Summaries are contained in F. S. Regs., Part II. and the Staff Manual respectively. Title Pages will be prepared in manuscript.

Place	Date	Hour	Summary of Events and Information	Remarks and references to Appendices
GINCHY. (near)	1	9 am to 4 pm	Intermittent fire on MOON + TREACLE trenches. Registration on enemy frontline in new Bde zone.	W.D.
		6 pm	Bursts of fire throughout the night on tracks between the BAPAUME Rd + ROCQUIGNY.	
	2	9 am	Day firing tasks as yesterday.	
		11.45	Under order from C.R.A. all guns in Bde retaliated with a burst of 5 rds gun fire on CEMETERY CIRCLE. ("ANSWER A.")	W.D.
		1.5 pm	Repeated on SUNKEN Rd (N 36.A) — "ANSWER B"	
			Several parties of enemy viewed N. of LE TRANSLOY + near BARASTRE at intervals during the day.	
	3	6 pm	Wind night firing.	
		9 am	Sweeping fire at intervals during day on enemy "supports". Saw rendezvous, registered on enemy frontline.	W.D.
	4	6 pm	Night firing as usual.	
		9 am	Day firing as yesterday.	
		2.30 pm	All guns in Bde retaliated with a burst of 5 rds gun fire on Sunken Rd. N. 30. d. S.O.I. has registered on new zone. 2 inch Junction registered. Howitzers in [?]. CEMETERY CIRCLE. — MSN TR. + vehicles on the ROCQUIGNY TRANSLOY Road. Bde took over new 3rd. extending from N. 36.d.7.1. to V.1.6.3.4.	W.D.
	5	4 pm	Night firing.	
		6 pm	Wind Day firing.	
		9 am		
		12.30 pm to 1.55 pm	Left Arty O.O. No. 9. Carried out — Bombardment Enemy Frontline to left of Bde zone. Further registration carried out. Usual night firing.	W.D.

WAR DIARY or INTELLIGENCE SUMMARY

Army Form C. 2118.

Place	Date	Hour	Summary of Events and Information	Remarks and references to Appendices
GINCHY. (near)	6.	9 am to 4 pm	Day firing at irregular intervals on MOON, STAR, & TREACLE Trenches. Registration of front line checked. Trench junctions registered; & BAPAUME Rd.	W.D.
		6 pm	Wind usual firing	
		12 mn	Heavy Artillery O.B. No 71. Carried out 40 min. bombardment of enemy front line. 18 pdrs searched C.T.s & till Khs.	W.D.
	7	1 pm to 4 pm	Registration of new Bangalore 3 on S.O.S. line from U.1.a.4.9 to N.3.S.c.8.8. Bde zone much assisted by bombardment of Left Artillery Group.	
		6 pm	Night firing as usual.	W.D
	8	9 am	MOON TRENCH searched by 18 pdrs. & SUNKEN Rd. N.30.d.5.4 Party of enemy observed in BAPAUME Rd dispersed by M.79. 4.5 Howitzers	W.D
	9	12.15 pm	Bombarding MOON TRENCH by Stokes. 18 pdrs. searched the bombarded area & SUNKEN Rd. in N.36.a. & N.30.d. shoot by pm on WINDMILL in D.31.b.	W.D
	10	6 pm	Usual night firing. Intermittent bursts of fire at stated times on special targets.	W.D
	11.	9 am	Intermittent fire on MOON. TREACLE & SYRUP TRENCHES. Registration of Rd junctions. Usual night firing. Day firing carried out as registration.	W.D

2449 Wt. W14957/Mgo 750,000 1/16 J.B.C. & A. Forms/C.2118/12.

Army Form C. 2118.

WAR DIARY
or
INTELLIGENCE SUMMARY

(Erase heading not required.)

Instructions regarding War Diaries and Intelligence Summaries are contained in F. S. Regs., Part II. and the Staff Manual respectively. Title Pages will be prepared in manuscript.

Place	Date	Hour	Summary of Events and Information	Remarks and references to Appendices
GINCHY (nun)	12.	8.30 a.m to 2 p.m	Normal day firing on enemy defences.	
		2.10 p.m	Left Arty. G.O. No 15 carried out. Bombardment by D/79 of BOSNIA TRENCH. Search bombardment area 2.10 to 2.50 p.m. of 79. Day firing resumed — night firing on back stg. & road.	Appx.
	13.	2.50		
		7.30 to 9.30 am	Registration enemy front line.	
		9.30	Burst Shrapnel on enemy defences.	
		12.40.	Left Arty G.O. No 14 carried out. 12.40 to 1.40 pm. Bombardment of portion of enemy front line in the front. by Stokes Mortars & trench & Vickers Rollings Barrage. Day firing resumed.	Appx.
	14.	1.40 9 am to 4 pm 5 pm	Normal day firing. Night firing. As yesterday.	Appx.
	15.		do	
	16	9. 4.30	Burst 9 pm fire at station turno + on special targets throughout the night.	Appx.
	17.		Normal day firing taken steps full power in early morning. Extra ammunition taken to make enemy tricks when Battery positions. Normal night firing.	Appx.
	18.		Normal day firing, observation improved owing to tunutar movements. Special night firing on trench areas at times I expected enemy relief.	Appx.

WAR DIARY or INTELLIGENCE SUMMARY

Army Form C. 2118.

Place	Date	Hour	Summary of Events and Information	Remarks and references to Appendices
GINCHY (near)	19.	9 am to 4 pm	18 pdrs carried out day firing on enemy defences. MOON TRENCH, SYRUP TRENCH, SOUTH ST., WINDMILL MOUND were all searched with bursts of fire. Night firing programme arranged. Known enemy runs by relief.	A.W.O.2
	20.		Day + Night. Enemy firing carried out as yesterday.	
	21.		Night. Enemy as usual. Got S.O.S call to all Batteries at 11 pm.	A.O.R.?
	22.	9 am 6 pm	Day firing on MOON, TREACLE + SYRUP TRENCHES by 18 pdr. + in front of LANDSTURM TRENCH. Knocking by B/79 in front of LANDSTURM TRENCH. Night. Enemy searchlights were seen by enemy relief. Bursts of fire the night.	A.O.R.?
	23.		Day. Enemy as yesterday. A/79 + B/79 cut wire at LANDSTURM TRENCH.	A.W.O.?
	24.		Knocking by all 18 pdr. Registration of special 3" standards in Left Battery Observation Area N°78. Considerable movement of enemy seamen in back areas.	A.W.O.?
	25.		Day. Enemy as usual. 300 pdr. Shrapnel fired at 7am. N. 36. d. Shots must interfered with enemy to hostile aeroplanes. Normal night firing.	A.O.R.?
	26.		Wire cutting continued.	
	27.	5.30 am	Operation Order N°78. The 87th Inf. Bde. 29th Dn. attacked a portion of the enemy front line + support trenches on a front of 1000 yds to a depth of 400 yds. 1st Borders on the Left. Inniskillings on Right. 18 pdrs started at Zero. 5.30 am with rolling barrage from our line 50 yds short of enemy front line. Rolling forward to a line 150 yds beyond the 2nd objective (ERSATZ POINT.) When standing barrage was maintained at varying rates of fire during period of consolidation. All Batteries stopped firing 9 to 12.30 pm 18 pdr. guns lack at photos opening the positions and dispersing them.	A.W.O.?

WAR DIARY or INTELLIGENCE SUMMARY

Army Form C. 2118.

(Erase heading not required.)

Place	Date	Hour	Summary of Events and Information	Remarks and references to Appendices
GINCHY (near)	28	5.15 pm & 6 am	2 rds from his to all Batteries and S.O.S. lines. During the day Batteries carried out registration of new S.O.S. lines. Friedhill on O.31.b. fired on, as movement was (seen).	A.W.1
		4.20 pm	2 Rds from his by all guns on S.O.S. lines in reply to enemy shelling on new trenches. During night, the tasks were to reach BAPAUME Rd. & Sunken Rd in Pole Zone.	
	29		Day firing on MOON & TREACLE TRENCHES. + searching fond shell Snipers were reported active. New S.O.S. line registered by all batteries. 4.5" How fired on a M.G. reported active at O.31.c.00.	W.W.2
	30		No firing from midnight 29-30 to midnight 29-30-31 by orders from Div Artillery H.Q.	W.W.3
	31	6.30 am	2 Batteries fired 4 rds from his on S.O.S. lines for retaliation at infantry request.	
		2.30 pm	All batteries fired 3 rds from his at request of infantry to retaliate for heavy hostile shelling of LANDSTURM TR. with 7.5 cm. Hns fired 30 Rds at hostile trench mortars.	W.W.4
		9.50 pm	All Batteries fired for 6 minutes on S.O.S. line as retaliation.	15 Apl/-

W.N. Thompson.
Lt. Col. R.M.A.
Cmdg. 79th I.A.B.

79th Brigade R.F.A.

War Diary for January 1917.

Appendix.

1. Ammunition expended during month of January.
   A. 10,010   AX. 20,050   BX. 8,730

2. Casualties during month of January.   Killed   Officers NIL   O.R. NIL
                                          Wounded "   NIL   O.R. NIL

3. Casualties to Horses: Killed   NIL   Wounded NIL
                           Died   3
                           Destroyed 14
   Destroyed Evacuated to Mobile Vet Section - 92.

4. Maltese from Schemes.   Officers 4.
                           O.R.   70.

W.J. Thompson.
Lieut. & Adjt.
for — Lt. Col. R.F.A.
Comdg. 79th Bde. R.F.A.

Army Form C. 2118.

WAR DIARY
or
INTELLIGENCE SUMMARY

FEBRUARY 1917.   79th BRIGADE R.F.A.

(Erase heading not required.)

Place	Date	Hour	Summary of Events and Information	Remarks and references to Appendices
GINCHY (near)	1.		18 pdr Batteries registered new S.O.S lines for "S.O.S. SOUTH" Howitzers registered enemy front line "BOSNIA" in U.1.d. & (searched) SUNKEN Rd in N.36.d for suspected Trench Mortar emplacements. Batteries in same position as last month. i.e.:— A/79 at T. 15.b. 1490 B/79 — T. 9.d. 1200 C/79 — T. 9.c. 6248 D/79 — T. 16.a. 0030	W97?
	2.	7.30pm	"L" B.Y R.H.A. (attached) at T.16.a.2.1. Gun Retaliation for enemy shelling in frontline. All Batteries opened a "slow barrage" on S.O.S. lines for 10 minutes.	
		5 am	On retaliation at infantry request all 18 pdrs fired 5 rds gun fire on S.O.S. line which proved effective.	
		11 am	A small party of the enemy observed at N.36.d.R.2. were fired on by "L" Bty. Infantry. Enemy observed at U.1.a. 4095 also fired on. Howitzers registered MOLTEN TRENCH in N.29.a. Registration of the pts by 18 pdrs.	W97?
		11.30 to 12.30 pm	Batteries gave a demonstration of S.O.S. barrage. Observed by G.O.C.R.A.	
		6.45 pm	18 pdrs fired 3 Rds gun fire on S.O.S. line in retaliation of infantry request.	
	3.	12.35 am	B/79 + C/79 "retaliated" on S.O.S. line 5 Rds gun fire at infantry request. C/79 registered MOLTEN TRENCH	W97?
		5.15 pm	50 Rds fired by 18 pdr "retaliation". Howitzers fired 30 Rds on MOLTEN TRENCH	
		7.45 am	S.O.S. Barrage great battery in checks by its respective F.O.Os from the frontline trench.	
	4.	9.20 pm	Howitzer fired instructed by enemy signals. A/79 barraged at slow rate for line N.36.d.9.3 — 3.R. at infantry request. Barrage effective.	W97?

Army Form C. 2118.

WAR DIARY
or
INTELLIGENCE SUMMARY.
(Erase heading not required.)

Place	Date	Hour	Summary of Events and Information	Remarks and references to Appendices
GINCHY. (near)	5.	5.25pm 6pm	A prearranged fire by batteries for calibration purposes. 16 pdr fired 30 rds HE on new trench N.36.a.6.6 re by way of retaliation. It was reported that enemy were extn. relieving or massing in MOON TRENCH in O.31.e. 4·5" Hows & one 18 pdr By fired bursts at this point for 30 minutes. Another 18 pdr By engaged new trench at N.36.a.6 re. Further an MOON TR. at N.36.b.	WD7
		11.30pm	18 pdr "retaliation" on NEW TRENCH & 4·5" Hows on MOON TRENCH O.31.e.	
	6.	1.3pm	Hostile report received 500 enemy collected at U.1.6.9.9. 3 18 pdr batteries at once switched to this target. Aeroplane reported "bursts O.K."	
		1.7pm 1.36pm	Another aeroplane tests completed with "prearr" satisfactn	WD7
		6pm	Night firing in burst by all batteries (harassing targets rept) to harass hostile working parties	
	7.		Registration carried on by all Batteries. T.M. emplacements and strong points engaged by A/79 at infantry request. 'L' R.H.A. fired on tracks to Return Trench, whips at intervals during night a trench junction	WD7
		9pm to 11pm	D/79 fired on Bailey Lane in accordance with O.O. 21 of lift artillery, W. whilst took on to cooperate with the Rifles-Group	
	8.	7.10am	Batteries fired W'W. alloted enemy trenches while the infantry attacked, capturing enemy position at SAILLY SAILLISEL. Operation successful.	
		6.15pm 6.40pm	Heavy barrage on our front line on 17 Divt front. All Batteries "stood to" to help "SOUTH Virginia". Bosche did not materialize. Firing kept up at intervals during night.	WD7

Casualties: 1 O.R. Wounded (G.S.W.) by 4·5" How. M.O. was hipped T.M.O.
3 36949 Sgt PARRY R. A/79. 96698 Dvr AGNEW J. A/79. 107192 Gnr GRAHAM E. B/79.

Army Form C. 2118.

WAR DIARY
or
INTELLIGENCE SUMMARY.
(Erase heading not required.)

Place	Date	Hour	Summary of Events and Information	Remarks and references to Appendices
GINCHY (nun)	9		All Batteries registered enemy lines from O.31.c.3.0 to N.36.d.8.2. Hostiles registered BOISNIL. Casualty 1. OR wounded GSW. 14795 Gnr WHEELER R.M. D/79	W.D.
		6 pm	Hostile shelling 18 pdr script H. BAPAUME Rd. How fire at intervals in dugouts in SUNKEN Rd N. 30.d.S.3.	
		10 pm	A/79 retaliates on hostile T.M. at N.36.6.7.2. with 30 Rds H.E.	
	10.	12.15 pm	Our 18 pdr batteries fire on S.O.S. line for "retaliation"	W.D.
		5.30 pm	Retaliation on MOLTEN TRENCH by 18 pdrs	
		2 pm	D/79 fires fire on V.I.A.5500 in retaliation with L/g arty O.O. 20 rpm Ell 2.53 pm. 2.B/79 RHA had 2 guns knocked out by direct hits from 15cm B.Fi. Were very busy carried out also "tests".	W.D.
	11.		4.5" How carried out an intermittent bombardment of trenches running back at O.31.c. 15 rds with good results.	W.D.
	12.		A/79 B/79 C/79 all calibrates 15-1 pm. WURTENBURG TRENCH destroying S.O.S. trench at	W.D.
	13.		D/79 bombarded 7.36.a.7.1. 50 Rds HE fired by 18 pdr v 60 Rds by Howitzers in T. Mortar in suspects influenced in N.36.a.76.	W.D.
		8.30 pm	Hostiles retaliates on T.M. in N.36.6. with 30 Rds.	
	14.	4.30 am	C/79 D/79 checked registration MOLTEN TRENCH.	W.D.
		9 am	B/79 fired a party of enemy seen in LUXEMBURG TRENCH	
		9 pm	Hostile mortar shelled T.M. post. 1 Section C/79 v 2 Section D/79 enfilade MOLTEN TRENCH until order to cease fire by Rocket sent up from ANZAC trenches at 9.25 pm. Raid successful: prisoners taken.	

WAR DIARY
or
INTELLIGENCE SUMMARY.
(Erase heading not required.)

Army Form C. 2118.

Place	Date	Hour	Summary of Events and Information	Remarks and references to Appendices
GINCHY (huts)	15	3 am	A/79 fired 70 Rds HE at Machine Gun in N.36.d with satisfactory results	WD?
		9 am to 4 pm	A/79 fired burst HE on enemy's new C.T. B/79 fired on hostile enemy Trench in WURTEMBURG TRENCH and WINDMILL C/79 fired on hostile T.M. reports active in O.26.b. Howitzer bombarded Trench junction & fired a fire gruney.	
		8 pm to 11.30.	Howitzer fired 12 gun salvoes in conjunction with D/78 on enemy Trench centers and finished shelling schedule time.	
	16		A few sniping rounds fired at enemy Howitzer Calibration carried out.	
		8.20 pm to 10 pm	B/79 ← A/79 fired 400 Rds HE in ERSATZ TRENCH + WURTEMBURG TR to even C/79 engaged enemy working parties dugouts new Trench. Casualties: 2. O.R. by enemy A.A. shell. (G.S.W) 42732 Cpl Aggott WH. } "L" B5. R.H.A. 95515 Gr. Rowlands N.F.	WD?
	17.		Rapid shoot in: visibility very low. Trench Mortar at N.36.6.1505 fired on by Howitzer & shrapnel	WD?
	18.	2.30 a.m. 4.30 a.m.	At dugouts reported Hours. fires. 36 Rds in N.36.6. " " " H.E. " " " on T.M. in MARS MINIE. 40 Rds " " " "	WD?
		10 p.m.	"L" RITA fired a burst of 50 Rds on hostile working party reports by infantry - party dispersed in N.36.d. - effect satisfactory.	
	19.	3.54 a.m 4.10 a.m	"L" RITA fired on SUNKEN Rd N.36.c, at 18 pm 8 mm the registration of Burris ? Batteries in hostile Trenches. Howitzer fired during the day on enemy defences.	
		5.40 pm	Howitzer ? Batteries (? Catch fusilliers ? & fired from all guns in the group and S.O.S. lines at various ? intervals from 7.12 pm. S.O.S. received from Right Battr. ? ? 10 minutes atont ? ? 7.50 pm ? ? Enemy captured "Pear B." when ? 6.20 pm	WD?

Army Form C. 2118.

WAR DIARY
or
INTELLIGENCE SUMMARY.
(Erase heading not required.)

Instructions regarding War Diaries and Intelligence Summaries are contained in F. S. Regs., Part II. and the Staff Manual respectively. Title pages will be prepared in manuscript.

Place	Date	Hour	Summary of Events and Information	Remarks and references to Appendices
GINCHY (near)	20.	10.30 am to 4.30 pm	WURTEMBURG, SAXON & MARS TRENCHES fired on at intervals by Stokes & Rifle Grenades and 18 pdrs kept up bursts of fire on hidden ground. Stokes & rifle grenades kept up all night for its same purpose without the support.	to 1/79
	21.	5 pm	13/79 Trn. Mortars bombarded ERSATZ TRENCH and MORTAR LANE to Posts "A" & "B" during the day. Stokes fired a slow barrage on MARS TRENCH and MORTAR LANE in retaliation for enemy T.M.	
		6.10 to 6.20 pm	L. RHA fired a "Slow barrage" on S.O.S. lines in support of the Rifle Brigade.	
	22.	12.30 pm	Large party of the enemy (seen moving along ERSATZ TRENCH): fire immediately brought to bear on them with good effect. Party dispersed. Another party seen near CEMETERY CIRCLE also dispersed. Another party seen near ANHALT TRENCH and bombarded "dead ground" interval during the day.	W/79
			A/79. Burst fire on MORTAR LANE. B/79. 6 fm. A/79. retaliation by H.E. penetrating bombs. D/79. 60 minutes with 3/78 in enemy 12-pm silence on MORTAR LANE T.M. Some movement of enemy observed. Our land moved effective retaliation. Met Sten. Sergt. HOLLAND H. killed. 1. O.R. wounded.	W/79
	23.	3.15 to 4.15	Some enemy firing.	
	24.		So so.. Nothing to report.	W/79
	25.	5.30 am	All 18 pdr Trn. retaliated on S.O.S. line for 30 mins. L.135 howitzers PRUSSIAN TRENCH, 3/79 bombarded enemy trenches in SUNKEN RD in N. 36. c. B/79 bombarded WURTEMBURG TRENCH.	W/79
		4.15 pm D/79	2 Other ranks... Lieut Masters... On Other half of Masters 39 31? Bn. TURNER TR. wounded Germ. No 153180. Bn. WILSON A. Killed (our still prisoners)	

Army Form C. 2118.

WAR DIARY
or
INTELLIGENCE SUMMARY.
(Erase heading not required.)

Instructions regarding War Diaries and Intelligence Summaries are contained in F.S. Regs. Part II. and the Staff Manual respectively. Title pages will be prepared in manuscript.

Place	Date FEB.	Hour	Summary of Events and Information	Remarks and references to Appendices
GINCHY (ruin)	26th	MIDI to 7am	18 pdrs reached trench and were instructed to fire on enemy in particular retiring from all the salients.	
		10 am to 5 pm	ANHALT and WURTEMBURG TRENCHES bombarded.	
		3.25 pm	At FOP (78th Bty) 18/79 fired to break up enemy party now reported forming in V.1.c.5.d.a.	ND
	27th	9am	"L" RIFT entered CEMETERY CIRCLE. Result unknown. Night – No 94597 Gnr DUNCALF P. wounded (GSW) No 94592 Gnr CORBETT A. (gas poisoning) wounded on 78th Bty. No 31353 Gnr DAVIS F. wounded (gas poisoning) Bnr Reliev 37362 Bar KING. 3 wounded — returns from front. Casualties for 26th –	NoD
		4 pm	# 8/75 put L.RHA bombarded ANHALT TRENCH J.T. D/79 bombarded PRUSSIAN TRENCH vicinity of 15th Inn Trenches. Night firing was instructed to Cemetery area.	NoD
	28th	5.25 am	Zero hr. attack by 104th K.R.R.C. on enemy posn in N.36.c. Left group Tank no 1 came out rolling barrages from its operation and mountain protection barrage; Division counter-attack. Rear group, Lat division tack, move unsuccessful. C/79 maintained protective barrage until 9 am. ERSATZ TRENCH.	NoD
		9 am	All batteries cease fire attempting regroup.	
		3.40 pm	18/79 engaged small hostile posn reported by D/78 in N.36.c.	
		8.30 pm	Hrs. opposite with D/78 in 12 gun salvos on T.M. in V.1.b. (At 2.30 pm, enemy shell "L".185 battery battery with four shell +4.2 Hrs. Capt. G.H. BAILEY (and) L RHA, Capt. D.A. GYE and 2 OR killed. + 4 OR wounded.) 3.OR wounded (gas still persistent)	
			D/79 Casualties : 141053 Gnr CARSON T. 61418 Gnr LAWSON C. 78375 Gnr WILSON W.H.	

W.H. Thompson Lieut Col
Lt-Col Comdg 79th Bde R.F.A.

Army Form C. 2118.

WAR DIARY
or
INTELLIGENCE SUMMARY.

(Erase heading not required.)

79th Bde. R.F.A.

Place	Date	Hour	Summary of Events and Information	Remarks and references to Appendices
			APPENDIX to War Diary for February 1917.	
		I	Ammunition expended during the month of January. A. 5494 AX 8820 BX 5864.	
		II	Casualties during month of January: Killed - Officer: NIL. O.R. 1; Wounded - Officer (attached) 2. O.R.(attached) 2. Officer NIL O.R. 13 Officer(attached) NIL O.R.(attached) 12. Wounded NIL	
		III	Casualties to Horses Killed - NIL — 11 Died - NIL Destroyed - 10 Evacuated (Mobile Vet. section) — 11	
		IV	Wastage from Sickness Officers NIL O.R. 65	

W.H. Thompson
Lieut. Col.
/Lieut Col. Comdg 79th Bde R.F.A.

WAR DIARY or INTELLIGENCE SUMMARY

Army Form C. 2118.

Place	Date	Hour	Summary of Events and Information	Remarks and references to Appendices
GINCHY (near)	1.	12 non	18 pdrs fired on and destroyed working party in CEMETERY CIRCLE.	WD?
	2.	10 pm	Howitzer fired on front German trenches in MARS AVENUS	
		5.10 am	Two 18 pdr Batteries fired a burst of 10 rds per gun fire at infantry request in S.O.S lines at CEMETERY CIRCLE.	
		10 am	Registration D.S.O.S. lines rgm hrs with Officer of relieving Brigade. Half Battery 79 FAB returns to Batteries G. 2 FAB. 79 FAB Batteries half the guns from Batteries respectively to 92nd Bde. Detachments returns proceeds to Wagon lines CARNOY.	WD
	3.		Relief of all Batteries completed by 2 pm. H.Q. moved to W.L. CARNOY. with remaining detachments of all Batteries	WD
	4.	8 am	Brigade nothing and chasing from at CARNOY. Advance parties sent to near W.L. near ALBERT. M. 29. a. 4. 5. to ALBERT — POZIERES Rd. Reconnaissance of new position by Bde Commander.	WD
	5.	7.30 am	Brigade marches to near Wagon lines via CARNOY - FRICOURT - BECORDEL and ALBERT.	WD?
	6.	2 pm	Reconnaissance by Battery Commanders.	
		3 am	6 guns B/79 and 5 guns D/79 went into action in following positions. B/79 at M. 28. a. 5075. C/79 at M. 28. a. 6580. D/79 at M. 27. b. 3555. O.P.o selected and wire run out. Group H.qrs (LColonel Kirk) at M. 31. c. 3.7.	WD
	7.		Batteries registered on GREVILLERS TRENCH and LOUPART TRENCH.	WD

Army Form C. 2118.

WAR DIARY
or
INTELLIGENCE SUMMARY.
(Erase heading not required.)

Instructions regarding War Diaries and Intelligence Summaries are contained in F. S. Regs., Part II and the Staff Manual respectively. Title pages will be prepared in manuscript.

Place	Date	Hour	Summary of Events and Information	Remarks and references to Appendices
ALBERT loupe line. guns at MARTINPUICH	8.		Registration continued.	1
	9.		do. do.	
		9.30.	Howitzer ammn. taken up to complete dump at guns of 300 Rds per How. B/79 had total ammn. and Div. Sgt. of one gun (?). 500 Rds per gun.	WD7
	10.	5.15 am 5.21	Zero Hour. Barrage opened intense. Infantry assaulted. Objective GREVILLERS TRENCH. Objective gained with little opposition. Casualties slight. Barrage very successful. Posts established in front of trench gained. Barrage lifted on to LOUPART TRENCH.	WD7
		5.30 am to 1.40 pm	Slow Barrage at irregular rate of fire on to LOUPART LINE. Infantry consolidated.	
	11.		A/79 in return attack. N.78 Div Artillery of R.H.A. carried (near MIRAUMONT) exchange guns with A/83. (18th Division)	WD9
			A.- B.- C./79 in action as above under inspection.	
			Group commander.	
	12.		do	WD9
	13.		Enemy retiring. Batteries firing extreme range.	
	14.		Batteries out of Range. Armed troops in minor AUBERT - BARONNE Rd.	WD9

WAR DIARY
or
INTELLIGENCE SUMMARY.

(Erase heading not required.)

Army Form C. 2118.

Instructions regarding War Diaries and Intelligence Summaries are contained in F. S. Regs., Part II. and the Staff Manual respectively. Title pages will be prepared in manuscript.

Place	Date	Hour	Summary of Events and Information	Remarks and references to Appendices
ALBERT Kaye Huts	15th	6.30 to 9.30	B/79 with two guns from position at MARTINPUICH D/79 withdrew their all returns to Kaye Huts ALBERT.	WD
MARTINPUICH Guns		9.30	All guns from that position removed to ALBERT-BAPAUME Rd. Kaye returned to W.L. full echelon. Casualties Wounded. 186938 Gr. DAY H.E. (G.S.W.) 10732 Dr. WILLS T. (G.S.W.) and 4 Kaye killed. – Enemy art of Troops.	WD
	16th	9.30	A/79 withdrew guns from R.H.A. Central to Kaye Huts.	
ALBERT	17th		All batteries withdrew from Kaye Huts at ALBERT cleaning + overhauling	WD
	18th	8.45 am	79th Bde marched from Kaye Huts at ALBERT to PUCHEVILLERS (14 miles) via BOUZINCOURT – TOUTENCOURT.	
PUCHEVILLERS	19th		Bde in billets in PUCHEVILLERS resting	WD
	20th	7.30 am	79th Bde marched to BEALCOURT – via – TALMAS – NAOURS – HAVERNAS – CANAPLES	WD
BEALCOURT	21st	9 am	14 guns to Heavy gun sent to 3rd Army Heavy Mobile Workshops – FREVENT for complete overhaul. Bde resting in billets.	WD
	22	"	"	
	23	"	"	
	24	11.30 am	Bde marched to the BOUBERS Artillery Area via WAVANS – VILLERS L'HÔPITAL – FORTEL – VACQUERIE to billets in CONCHY-SUR-CANCHE. All vehicles advanced one hour 11 pm became 12 midnight. (ARMY ORDER)	WD
	25	11 pm 6 am	79" Bde (less gun teams, limbers & personnel for same) marched to ST MICHEL (about 12 miles)	WD
ST MICHEL			into billets near ST POL.	
	26.	3 pm	79" Bde marched to a camp S.W. of BRAY (near ARRAS) via AUBIGNY + ACQ. Transport was sent in advance at 12.30 pm. – distance about 17 miles.	WD
BRAY.	27	9.30 am	Bryce motor canvas at Reconnaissance of positions near St CATHERINE at G. 3. c. Central. Reconnaissance by Battery Commanders of positions. (Maps 51.B. N.W.) HQrs at G. 2. b. Central.	WD

Army Form C. 2118.

WAR DIARY
or
INTELLIGENCE SUMMARY.
(Erase heading not required.)

Place	Date	Hour	Summary of Events and Information	Remarks and references to Appendices
BRAY.	28th	9.30 am	Working parties continued to prepare A/79 & B/79 each took out 4 Npas guns of 160" Bde RFA in positions for the purpose of recruiting. C & D/79 dug out new positions. A B & C/79 sheet 57 b. Work on positions continued. C & D/79 sheet 57 b. C.P.s elected.	App
	29th	6 pm	Guns of A, B & D/79 returns to Wagon Lines from 3rd Army workshops.	App
	30th		Work on positions continued — wire cutting by B & A/79. 250 Rds per Bty for this	
		7 pm	Guns of A & B of D/79 taken up into action.	App
	31st	7 pm	Guns of C/79 returns from 3rd Army workshops. 6 Guns of 160" Bde withdrawn from vicinity of Wagon Lines. Skilled artillerie brigade up by 15cm gun.	App

D.W. Crofton
Lieut-Col. R.F.A.
Cmdg. 79th F.A.B.

WAR DIARY
or
INTELLIGENCE SUMMARY

(Erase heading not required.)

79th F.A.B.

Army Form C. 2118.

Place	Date	Hour	Summary of Events and Information	Remarks and references to Appendices
			APPENDIX	
			To War Diary for March 1917.	
		I	Ammunition expended during the month of March 1917. (Approx.) A 5520 4 x 3755 15 x 1675	
		II	Casualties during month of March. Killed :- NIL 1 OR. Wounded :- 2 OR.	
		III	Casualties to Horses. Killed :- 4 Wounded :- NIL Lost NIL. Died or Destroyed :- 29 Evacuated to Mob. Vet. Sectn. 22	
		IV	Wastage from Sickness Officers. NIL O.R. 64.	

Army Form C. 2118.

WAR DIARY
or
INTELLIGENCE SUMMARY.
(Erase heading not required.)

79th F.A.B. APRIL 1917

Places	Date	Hour	Summary of Events and Information	Remarks and references to Appendices
"C" Camp S.W. of BRAY.	1st		A/79 & B/79 in position near ST CATHERINE - knocking in enemy wire & front line - and attack to 760th Bde 32nd Divl Arty. C/79 from front sub-fortress attacked A-B/79. Continued bombarding enemy defences Casualties April 1st (Amm² Terra)	Appx 1
	2		D/79 Do Do Defences wounded D² NICHOLLS E. 124216 S/S BRAY M.B. killed 26840 D² BUCHANAN N. 80932 D² BAIRNES J. 6929 D² HASLER H. 979.05 " JONES W.R. 55357 G² BATCUP J. 14656 " JACKSON H. 14388 1330 " VERO F. 74597 " DUNCAN E. (wounded) 133646 " MOIR A.(since died of wounds).	Appx 2
	3			Appx 3
	4th		AREAS OPERATIONS began ("V" Day) Bombardment by heavy field trench Howitzers by 18 Pdrs and T.M.s	Appx 4
	5th	8 am	"W" Day As above - Practice Barrage - movement too light.	Appx 5
	6th	11 am	"X" Day Practice Barrage.	Appx 6
	7th	11.15	"Q" Day Practice barrage - very satisfactory. Casualty wounded No 55755 Sergt GROOME J.	Appx 7
	8th	11.15 am	Y. Day short practice barrage.	Appx 8

WAR DIARY
or
INTELLIGENCE SUMMARY.

(Erase heading not required.)

Army Form C. 2118.

Place	Date	Hour	Summary of Events and Information	Remarks and references to Appendices
ST CATHERINE	9th		"Z DAY"	
BRAY Wggn		5.30 am	ZERO HOUR.	
			Line located at 8 am.	
		8 am	"A" Sub.com. (5 F.B. Wggn pair Bty) moves to "Rendezvous at Marks" ((G.20.d.4.4))	
			"B" Sub.com. and attacks D.A.C. transport machine to AGNEZ to open at 8.13 Division	
		5.30am	Guns intense Barrage, transported by succession to left E exhibit 1.14 p.m.	
		5.34	Infantry assaulted: "BLACK LINE" forward 8.25 B. Group J	
		8.13 pm	" " and took "BLUE LINE" Duncan E	
		1.15 pm	All guns pulled out of position and joined remainder of "A" Echelon at "Rendezvous"	
		6 am	at G.20.A.4.4	
		6.30 pm	"A" Echelon took the position on the line of march on the DOULLENS – ARRAS Rd	
		11 am	Rey advance Guard Battery behind the 9th Northumberland Fusiliers.	
			29/74 : B & C/79 marched in order named behind the Duke of WELLINGTON Regt	
			Hd.qrs. D/79.	
ARRAS		9.0 pm	Division halted for tonight, taking any cover available where they halted.	
		11.15	At H. Qrs of N° of R.D. Brig. H.qrs at G.36.d.3.0. The remainder Battery in reserve	
			1st GARE DU NORD. Brig. H.qrs at G.26 W.3.4.5 Batteries under strength at reserve in J.26	
			52 B.H. Brig-General CLARKE.	
	10th		Brigade in several H.qr lines under 30mm notice to march.	
		11.15 am		

Army Form C. 2118.

WAR DIARY
or
INTELLIGENCE SUMMARY.

(Erase heading not required.)

Instructions regarding War Diaries and Intelligence Summaries are contained in F. S. Regs., Part II. and the Staff Manual respectively. Title pages will be prepared in manuscript.

Place	Date	Hour	Summary of Events and Information	Remarks and references to Appendices
ARRAS	11		Brigade in same positions. Under 1 hour notice to move.	
	12.	10.15 am	Bde received orders from VI Corps releasing the 11th Div. Artillery (Sgt* Inf3)	
		11 am	Reconnaissance of position by Bde & 43 acting Commanders. Gun of 59th InB taken and in pits stripped except for overnight & ammunition pits. 79th InB handed over item from to 5.28.816 in ARRAS.	W12
		7 pm	79th RFA took over defence of this from SG* Bn; 3rd Div. Art. 17th Div Arty took over orders of 1st 3rd Div. Arty	
	13.		O.P.c manned during the hours of daylight. Casualties 2 O.R. killed. OP N.4.a.3.6 No 141056 Gnr CASSON. T.J 3/73 94599 Gnr CORBETT A. J 3/73	W13
		7 am	Registration by 3rd Division to Captain GUEMAPPE.	
		6.20 pm	Quantin by 3rd Division to Captain GUEMAPPE. Infantry attack 79th Bde opened intense barrage. Enemy forward to East of village from 6.44 pm	
		7 pm	16.7 hrs Enemy entered the village but were driven out. 30S reports success doubtful.	
		5.7 pm	2.17 reports Counter unsuccessful – barrage reopened 300 yds E. of GUEMAPPE	W14
		8.20 pm	Barrage from 1 gun E. of RAVINE in 0.13.d. Guns left returned to support him.	
		9.27 pm	Hens lands in 0.13.d.	
		9.50.	Bde stopped firing.	
	14.	5.30 am	To assist 29th Infantry attack of Hill 100 in 0.2.d. 79th Bn opened concentrated barrage across the CAMBRAI Rd until 6.50 am. Objective found but infantry held in trenches under heavy counter attack in 0.7.d.2.6 by 4h75.	W14
		13.10 pm	Party of enemy seen massing near factory in Hoofe-de-la-fosse. O.R. N556/3/K. BARBER H. 9/75 dispersed by our movement. Gun WAPPER JW. (B/r4) 196373. Gnr LAMBERT R. (GSW)

14556 Gn
A8534 W. W.4073 M887 750,000 8/16 D D & L Ltd. Forms/C2118/13.

WAR DIARY or INTELLIGENCE SUMMARY

Army Form C. 2118.

Place	Date	Hour	Summary of Events and Information	Remarks and references to Appendices
MONCHY LE-PREUX	15th		Casualties: Reputedly 1 newS.O.S. line. Mails 16. Mar. Cur Fulke took over command. Eck CASTLE to (G.H. Northumberland Fusiliers). N.E. of MONCHY cnemy 10"S.L." INF. BN. Battery considerably trailed by gas shelle. No orphans.	WAD
	16th	9 am	Reputedly. Various points on new Bn. KEELING COPSE + CROSS RD. I 25 d 79. 1 O.R. killed by shell at gun position. 36633 Gnr. BOULTON W. 7/B/79. No 2 F.F 2H Gnr BAINS G. (A/76). 109603 Gnr WRIGHT T. 3/79.	WAD
		8 pm	18 pdrs. Searched the MONCHY - PELVES Rd. throughout the night with twenty firs and through new some searches to the Battery. Slow Barrage for S.O.S. Sent up by Duvinin and night 1 O.R. D/79. 145256 Gnr NAPPER J. 20 minutes in support. Casualties wounded	WAD
	17th	8.15 pm	Parties of enemy observed and fired on trying to bring in wounded Capt. William Nigel MacKenzie M.C. 3/B/79. Casualties 2 O.R. Killed out of range.	WAD
			36534 Dr. HOPLEY J. 299.23 G.C. HOLDEN 3 0/79. 36637 Dv. DAVIES D 104942 Gr. M. EDWARDS 3 D/79.	
	18		Battery orders to increase every pm. Casualties. Heavy hostile shelling attempt to S.O.S. in pm. MASR W/H GOSSE ME wounded. 18387 Dr KAY J A/79. Night Guns carried out Searches with burst pm 3573 Gr BISSETT C. A/79. 6th to MONCHY - PELVES Road killed Bv DOYLE B/79 51140 Gr NEWTON W.S. D/79. 9/53rd Gr KNIBBS A.J. D/79.	WAD
	19	2.65 am 7 am	Battery again heavily shelled at intervals during the day with 5.9 in 4.2 in Heart. Reconnaissance for new positions in N.4.b by Bde + Battery Commanders and new Battery position found. A/79 H.3.4.C.S.8. B/79 N.4.b.S.R. C N.4.b.35.80. CASUALTIES 1/Lt. J.L. KERSHAW 3 0/79. B.S.M. BEAMS C.H.H 1/44 Dr B. SIMMONS J D/79. 86401 Dv GEE E. D/79.	WAD

WAR DIARY
or
INTELLIGENCE SUMMARY.

Army Form C. 2118.

Place	Date	Hour	Summary of Events and Information	Remarks and references to Appendices
MONCHY	20		Registration carried out by all Batteries. Casualties. Killed. No T/15793 Gr. FINDLAY. S. D/79 Killed 87583 Dr. SHIPLEY. J.H. (C/79) Wounded 93806 Gr. HATCH. S. 16051 Gnr. BURDEN R. } A/79 Dies of Wounds 46841 B.S.M. BEAMS C.H.H. 11719 Gnr EVANS H.J. (D/79)	W/79
	21.		Harassing Fire throughout the day. Kept up by all batteries on enemy tracks roads & villages. Casualties Wounded Registration continues. 1/36645 a/Bdr. BARKER. A.S. } 3/79 Major HORNSBY 7th men command 9/8/79. 37856 Sergt. CURRIE J. } D/79 138911 Gnr. MARRALL. J.	W/79
	22.	7 pm	Harassing Fri. continued all day & night. Practice Barrage. D/79 bombarding enemy batteries throughout the night with lachrymatory & B× shell. Heavy hostile fire Hooplet Wd	W/79
	23.		Casualties Killed 138797 Gnr. BAKER E. (C/79) Wounded 53329 Dr. SAWYER. C.E. (C/79) 92935 Dr. ANDERSON R. A/79 20965 Dr. FALKLAND G. 116037 Br. HOTCHKIS "A" D/79 Dr. MEEK P. D/79 Br. Brown on Right.	
		4.45 am	17th 57th & 29th Division attacks. 17th Division covered by 33rd & 17th Divl. Artillery. 2nd 26d Hour. 17th Division concentrated by 73rd. kept up by M.G. fire. 57th Inf. Bde assaulted 1st Objective. 5. Staff & Lyff. Bde after to take 1st Objective. Lyft C/B REED (A/79) Liasn Officer with Rifle Bdn. Continuous bombardment by all Batteries at varying rates/min. a appendix	W/79
		N	S.O.S. line until 5.07 pm.	
		6.0 pm	Re-became bombard'mt. Enemy Trench rays long to 1st Objective. Artillery 10th up support SOS lime	

WAR DIARY or INTELLIGENCE SUMMARY

Army Form C. 2118.

Place	Date	Hour	Summary of Events and Information	Remarks and references to Appendices
MUNCHY	23.	7.30 pm	Slow rifle & Vickers kept up in S.O.S. lines.	WWO
		9.10 pm	S.O.S. all Battns.	
		9.15 pm	Situation made normal. Rate of fire slowed down.	
		9.25 pm	Battns. stopped firing.	
		9.50 pm	A/79 received burst of rifle & M.G. fire.	
		10.30 pm	Night firing from own trench. Have on SHELL TRENCH.	
			Casualties: 9327/3 Bdr. ELGIN C.O. } wounded
			28644 a/Bdr PICKERING A.E. } 9/79
			798 Dr. HERON D. 9/79 Killed.	
24.			Registration of RIFLE + BAYONET TRENCHES	
			Quiet Day.	
			Casualties: Killed 108687 G: CARPENTER G. (9/79)
			200015 G: WOOD W. (B/79) WWO
			Dr LOVE J. "	
			Wounded 97617	
		10 pm	Night firing on own trench areas.	
25		3.30 am ZERO	52nd Inf Bde assaults RIFLE + BAYONET TRENCHES without preliminary bombardment.	
		3.40	Barrage all 18pdr batteries at new S.O.S. lines. (Protection Barrage) Return	
		3.50	Barrage 2 mins per zone for 6 mins.	
		4.10 am	Occupied huts & pen beyond of huts	
			Regt. Bttn. (Manchester Regt.) took their objective.	
			Left Bttn. (West Riding) failed owing to M.G. fire.	
		10.30 am	13/79 engages new enemy trench with bursts of fire, also track batteries.	WWO
		1 pm	Stores consolidated Northern flank BAYONET TRENCH	
		8 pm	Casualties.	
		10 pm	12th Division relieved 17th Division. 35th Bde relieved 52nd Bde.
			A/79 Night firing on track batteries	

Army Form C. 2118.

WAR DIARY
or
INTELLIGENCE SUMMARY.
(Erase heading not required.)

Instructions regarding War Diaries and Intelligence Summaries are contained in F. S. Regs., Part II. and the Staff Manual respectively. Title pages will be prepared in manuscript.

Place	Date	Hour	Summary of Events and Information	Remarks and references to Appendices
MONCHY	26.	9 am to 7 pm	Observed fire on working parties & enemy new trenches. Registration carried out by Hows.	WM9
		9 pm	Burst of gun fire during night in approaches.	
	27	9 am	Howitzers harassed enemy's trenches.	
		11.30 am	A/74 reported CARTRIDGE TRENCH by aeroplane & satisfactory. Visibility too low for further observation.	KM2 D/74 SMITH A
		9 pm	Night firing on approaches.	
	28	4.25 am	Zero Hour. Attack by 35th Inf Bde (12th Division) on BAYONET & RIFLE TRENCHES. 7th Norfolks on the Right, 5th Royal Berks on the Left. 15 minutes barrage 200 yds beyond the 1st Objective, 10 minutes with then advanced in rushes of 50 yds. Beyond the SOS. line. 1st Objective captured by each battalion. Ind. batt battalions pushed to 2nd Objective 500 yds beyond its first one. Heavy M.G. fire. 7th Norfolks were pushed back at RIFLE TRENCH. A protective barrage was kept up at rapid rate for 1 hr into 112 min. Several parties of the enemy were observed moving down from the morning.	WM1
		12 noon		
		8 pm	Troops in approaches.	
	29.		Bombardment of the portion of RIFLE TRENCH lost by the enemy also all new trench left under searching fire throughout the day.	WC

Army Form C. 2118.

WAR DIARY
or
INTELLIGENCE SUMMARY.

(Erase heading not required.)

Instructions regarding War Diaries and Intelligence Summaries are contained in F. S. Regs. Part II. and the Staff Manual respectively. Title pages will be prepared in manuscript.

Place	Date	Hour	Summary of Events and Information	Remarks and references to Appendices
MONCHY.	30	3.30 a.m.	7/1 Norfolks attacked the putting of RIFLE TRENCH shelled led by its enemy. 18 pm held up protected ourselves and S of line Monymore RIFLE TRENCH for 1 hour. Attack successful.	App 1
		4.30 a.m	Our infantry bombs and RIFLE TRENCH again 7 am Rifle Trench. Information from all Bty by all Batteries to also C.T. laden up to same.	
		7 pm	Enemy now trench held were hurricane fire - thought by heavy shelling of A/79. Prov. by a 5.9 m 7B5 at interval of throughout the day. Answered No 72092. Gm. REYNOLDS. W. B/79.	

W.H. Thompson.
Lieut ??
for Major cmdg 79th F.A.B.

WAR DIARY
INTELLIGENCE SUMMARY

79th F.A.B.

APPENDIX

I. War Diary for April 1917.

Ammunition expended during the month of April 1917.
Shrap. A. 49562 A× 27773 B× 13,114 Gas 1069.

II. Casualties during the month of April.
Killed: Officers nil. O.R. 15
Wounded: Officers 3. 43
and 1 A.S.C. driver attached killed
— 27. nurse 7.

III. Casualties to horses
Killed
Died on Destroyed 63
Evacuated to Mobile Vet. Section 80.
O.R. 4c 4c.

IV. Wastage from sickness: Officers 2. O.R. 4c 4c.

W.H. Thompson
Lieut.Col.
Adjutant Comdg 79th F.A.B.

WAR DIARY
or
INTELLIGENCE SUMMARY

Army Form C. 2118.

79th F.A.B.

MAY 1917

Place	Date	Hour	Summary of Events and Information	Remarks and references to Appendices
MONCHY-LE-PREUX	1st	4 A.M.	18 pdrs opened Barrage on S.O.S. lines. Carried out a slow drill bombardment for 8 mins (intense). Heavy retaliation until 4.45 am from midnight until 3 am. Enemy gas shell into BOIS DU SART. Remainder of day quiet, except for heavy hostile shelling on our approaches. 7th East Surreys.	A/3
	2nd	1.1 a.m.	18pdrs attacked to [portion] of RIFLE TRENCH held by the enemy. Before intended shelling "barrage" on S.O.S. line, the slow barrage for 1 hour. Trench captured then neighbours to the enemy. Practice barrage (slow & creeping) by all Batteries for operation on 11.3 a.m.	A/3
		3.65 p.m.		
		8.30.	Bombardment of BOIS DU SART dugouts by D/79 with chemical shell.	
	3rd	3.45 A.M.	Zero Hour. 1st, 3rd & 5th Armies attacked at zero. 36th & 37th Bdes & 2/12th Divisions attacks between MONCHY — RIVER SCARPE. 79th & 78th Fd.Bdes. covered the advance of 37th Bde with a creeping Barrage. 1st BROWN LINE. (1st objective.) (6th Battn. the Buffs on Right and 2nd East Surreys left supports by 2nd West Kents and 6th Queens in reserve. 18 pdr Barrage commenced intense rate a S.O.S. line, then crept forward to a [?] barrage line 200 yds beyond it. 1st Objective. Elements of 6th BUFFS reached these under our barrage. Enemy massed up counter attacks with supporting heavy troops from our protective barrage he succeeded in driving our back to ARROW TRENCH (with [except] a small party who succeeded in holding portion of	A/3

Place	Date	Hour	Summary of Events and Information	Remarks and references to Appendices
NOYON (Contd)	3 (Contd)		CARTRIDGE TRENCH all Bn + 2 companies held GUN TRENCH all Nyt. These elements threw withdrawn at night 15 RIFLE TRENCH. During the day several parties attempted moving for counter-attack were observed & stopped up by Artillery. Counter-attack thought of by 35 with right Bn (6th Buffs(?)) extremely difficult to maintain.	6/40
		3.50 am	On 14S Hants. Dyk. (Karma up by permanship killed 1 offr M/S 3376 Sgt PEDDAR J ? and Transky 1 OR. No 3076 Sgt. NODDSHOPOFN T.(killed) M/S3345 Sgt. PEDDAR J.(wounded) Hostile fire on batteries very light—mostly concentration on ??? infantry.	
		9.4?	2/ Bn attempts again to go forward. Enfiladed M.G. fire. Attack arm half-???? from M.G. fire ? the mountains. Protection brought through the grenade—79 Bn. 378 Bn. have been freed further by M.5 fire. Considered to	
		6 am	RIFLE TRENCH — SCABBARD TRENCH but 18 Ph manage to establish ??? beyond this line even by element it is not considered repeats complete in dmn ??? ??? very great.	WF
		4.30 am	Remained in ??? line Russians wounded remaining	

WAR DIARY / INTELLIGENCE SUMMARY

Army Form C. 2118.

Place	Date	Hour	Summary of Events and Information	Remarks and references to Appendices
MONCHY	5		Bursts of fire received put down on hostile positions of enemy defences. No movement observed.	WA?
	6		do	WA?
	7	7.20 pm	do. Enemy shelled our trenches heavily for 20 mins. No attacks developed.	WA?
			Calibration + Registration carried out. Small parties enemy put in Constructing position.	WA?
	8		All Batteries continued Registration.	WA?
	9		do	WA?
	10		Major L.S. Warren took over command of the Brigade from Major F.H. Hornell	WA?
			returned to B/74. Quiet day. Except for Registration, little firing from our artillery.	WA?
	11		Received hints of an outbreak "GRENADIER WINCHES"	WA?
		9.30 pm	Harassing fire kept up all night Search. Bryant Bn Battalions. Smythe Burrage L Bn SCARPE VALLEY firing. 8th attd at 4.14 Div in Chemical works.	WA?
	12	6.30 am	Intense fire on enemy front line. No movement followed by 20 minute short bursts in support trenches.	WA?

Army Form C. 2118.

WAR DIARY
or
INTELLIGENCE SUMMARY.
(Erase heading not required.)

Place	Date	Hour	Summary of Events and Information	Remarks and references to Appendices
MONCHY-LE-PREUX	13th	9.14 p.m	Heard Iry firing in trenches S.O.S. reported to have gone up on our front.	WD?
		9.22 p.m	79th Bn front line Lewis Gun officer reports all quiet	
	14th		Heard Inf firing high — during day reports of several enemy aeroplanes observed within range, fire first on enemy movement observed within a close. Bombardment	WD?
	15th	3 p.m	All Battery tgts handed in — enemy movement observed taking enemy lines. Orders received from CRA 12th Div. to withdraw guns to W.P.Z. on night of 15/16.	WD?
		3 p.m	Reconnaissance of new position in front of FONTAINE-LES-CROISILLES and men to HENIN-SUR-COJEUL, by B.C. Commander and B.C's	WD?
		5 p.m	Bde Salvo fired into to Bois du Sart.	
		8.30 p.m 11.30	Guns withdrawn to Wagon lines at MARET.	
	16th	9 a.m	HQrs moved to Wagon lines MARET. Batteries marched independently to HENIN via MERCATEL & ADINT BECQUERELLE took up positions in SUNKEN Rd in T.3.B. from T.3.15.7.2 to T.7.3.6.4.6.	WD?
HENIN-SUR-COJEUL	17th	11 am	Bde Hqrs at T.3.a.1.8. Batteries established communication with O.P. & reported own noted in U. & B.	WD?
		4 p.m	Day spent in registration & consolidating gun position. Ammn brought up to 500 rds per gun.	

WAR DIARY
INTELLIGENCE SUMMARY

Place	Date	Hour	Summary of Events and Information	Remarks and references to Appendices
HENIN.	18th		Registration continued. Working parties on work carried on at gun positions.	WATT
	19th		do do	
	20th	5.15 am	Zero Hour. 33rd Div. attacks a portion of the HINDENBURG LINE between FONTAINE-LES-CROISILLES and the CROISILLES-HENDECOURT Road. 98th Bde attacks in left. 100th Bde Centre. 19th Bde on Right. 2y² Bn RFA. cooperates by forming a smoke barrage at the South West end of FONTAINE to screen the assault from Hostile M.G.s. D/77 forms smoke barrage M.S.?	WOO
		5.40 am	HINDENBURG FRONT LINE captured at Berg. HINDEN BURG Support Line then attacked but held up by M.G. fire	
		10.30 am	Situation reported as certain. HINDENBURG FRONT LINE captured throughout with prob Probs cut in front.	
		7.15 am to 9.45 am	Protective Barrage on SOS line at varying rate 4/gun.	
		9.15 am	Hostile 4.5 How Bty. Hostile M.G. fire in support of. Hostile Bty. appears to be trying to enfilade M.G. at U.7.B.7.7	
		11 am	Party of enemy reported to be digging in 18 pdr and 4.5 How.	
		11.25 am	Thornycroft ammunition lorry ? ? much movement observed. fired on when within range	

A5834 Wt. W4973 M687 750,000 8/16 D. D. & L. Ltd. Forms/C.2118/13.

Army Form C. 2118.

WAR DIARY
or
INTELLIGENCE SUMMARY.

(Erase heading not required.)

Instructions regarding War Diaries and Intelligence Summaries are contained in F.S. Regs., Part II. and the Staff Manual respectively. Title pages will be prepared in manuscript.

Place	Date	Hour	Summary of Events and Information	Remarks and references to Appendices
HENIN-SUR-COJEUL	20	7.30 PM	Second attack launched to capture the HINDENBURG SUPPORT. 18 pdr barrage moving back on objective of HINDENBURG SUPPORT – & bombarded HINDENBURG SUPPORT – @	WD?
		7.40 PM	Hour lifted on to Railway cutting from FONTAINE	
		8 PM	The first 18 pdr shrapnel burns carry back portion of HINDEN BURG SUPPORT captured	WD?
	21	3.30 AM	S.O.S. reported to have been sent up on our front. Batteries opened up intense fire for 10 mins. then slow rate of fire. During the day 18 pdrs engaged CORPS TARGETS with HE and 4.5 How howitzers bombarded enemy dugouts in Bde Zone. Ammunition dump at front opened. Wrapping up supplies per gun	WD?
	22		Quiet day – a few stray rounds fired.	
		7.15 pm	Guns reduced by one to interference batteries at Bryan Lanes at MOYENVILLE. Ammn at front landed over to 74th FAB.	WD?
	23	9.30	A/79 & B/79 withdrew guns	
		10.30	C/79 & D/79 " " in MENIN	
		10 am	High command at MENIN. 79 Bde marched to Battery Wagon lines ARRAS. A 4/8/79 at BOISVILLE. C & D/79 in G.26.a. (G.34.a 2.7.) RWF DEC. BAPDETS AREA	WD?
ARRAS.		1 pm	HQrs at No.1 RWF DEC Bapdets Area wagon line G.28.d.2.4 Batteries resting.	

WAR DIARY or INTELLIGENCE SUMMARY

Army Form C. 2118.

Place	Date	Hour	Summary of Events and Information	Remarks and references to Appendices
ARRAS	24.		Battery (returning) of Battery Junction near FEUCHY CHAPEL. Reconnaissance of Battery Junction near FEUCHY CHAPEL.	WD
	25.	1 am	Orders received to take up 2 16/79 Batteries + 2 Section D/ Stores into action on 28th inst.	WD
		7 pm	A + C/79 to details. B/79 + D/79 took up all their guns but nothing personal removed at W.T.	WD
		4 pm	Hdqrs established at N.2.b. 8050. Communication established with all Batteries. L.Col. WARREN 16th arm Command of the Group, 79th + B/or	
MONCHY (new)	26.		Registration carried out by A C + D/79 on HOOK TRENCH - THE MOUND and BOIS DU VERT - 79th in vicinity of MONCHY CHURCH Btties took up positions of the line held by 81st Inf. Bde. 79th Bde. took over Russian supplies with the Right Battn. (2nd Royal Fusiliers) 29th Division.	WC
		6 pm	L.Col. RIDDLE took over command of 17th D.A. Group	WD
	27th		Night firing on approaches + tracks by all Batteries. Harassing fire kept up by D/79 carrying out interdictor shoot on HOOK D/79 in cooperation with ... TRENCH - much damage done.	WD
			Left from carried out on enemy patrols at specified hours. Have negative BOIS DU VERT by Right Battn. satisfactorily.	WD
	28.		Enemy in retaliation. Have registered HOOK + LONG TRENCHES.	
	29.		18 pdr harassing fire on enemy defenses. Nylr. Farm - Silver on S.O.S. line during the night.	Casualties Wounded 2 OR. GSW. No 91760 Gnr POSTEVIN W/ 5/79 No 58103 Gnr HADLEY T/ 8/79 WD

WAR DIARY
or
INTELLIGENCE SUMMARY.
(Erase heading not required.)

Army Form C. 2118.

Instructions regarding War Diaries and Intelligence Summaries are contained in F. S. Regs., Part II. and the Staff Manual respectively. Title pages will be prepared in manuscript.

Place	Date	Hour	Summary of Events and Information	Remarks and references to Appendices
MONCHY - LE-PREUX.	30.		Harassing Fire throughout day on trench and battery posts.	
			Registration 1 HOOK TRENCH by 18 pdrs.	AAA
			Bombardment of LONG TRENCH by 4.5" Hows.	
		11.30 pm (Zero)	Hostile battery opposite active. Infantry action by additional assault by D/79. HOOK TRENCH. (1st/1st Middlesex Regt on Right 2nd Royal Fusiliers on centre)	
		11.30	18 pdrs 4.5 Hows intense barrage	
		11.34	Lyddite 100x	
		11.36	Shrap 100x } then formed protective barrage.	
			Objectives gained by 86th Bde. Intense m.g. & rifle fire from opposing Strongpoints. Counter-bombardment slight.	
			Protective barrage carried on till 1pm kept up until 2 am	
	31.	2.0 am	Normal night firing resumed.	
		9 am	Reconnaissance portion of HOOK TRENCH lost.	MMQ
			Enemy reported occupying BOIS DU AUBERPINES.	
		10.0 am	18 pdr uses "COUNTER PREPARATION.	
		10.30 pm	Normal day firing resumed. Battery positions visits by GOC RA 3rd ARMY.	
			B/79, detachment withdrawn to range line.	
			1 Section D/79. " "	
			Night quiet.	

W.H. Thompson

Lieut. & Adjutant,

79th FAB.

Army Form C. 2118.

WAR DIARY
May 1917
INTELLIGENCE SUMMARY
APPENDIX (Erase heading not required.) 75th FA.B

Instructions regarding War Diaries and Intelligence Summaries are contained in F. S. Regs., Part II. and the Staff Manual respectively. Title pages will be prepared in manuscript.

Place	Date	Hour	Summary of Events and Information	Remarks and references to Appendices
		I	Ammunition expended during month of May. A. 18230. AX 10815. BX 10210. CHEMICAL 78th SMOKE.	1010.
		II	Casualties during month of May. Killed: Officers. NIL. O.R. 1 Wounded: Officers NIL. O.R. 5. wounds at duty O.R. 5.	
		III	Horses from Sickness. Officers. 1. O.R. 49.	
		IV	Casualties to Horses. Killed & destroyed. 9. Died. 4. Lost. 1. Evacuated to M.V.S. 13.	

W H Hampson
Lt Col
75th FA Bde

WAR DIARY
INTELLIGENCE SUMMARY
for 79th Brigade R.F.A.
June 1917

Army Form C. 2118.

Place	Date	Hour	Summary of Events and Information	Remarks and references to Appendices
MONCHY LE PREUX	June 1 1917		Normal night and day firing throughout 24 hours. 45 Hours bombard to LONG TRENCH - 100 Rds	MM
	2		do	MM
	3	1 pm	C.R.A. 3rd Divn Artly took over command of the 17th, 33rd & 29th Artillery (covering 3rd Division) from 29th CRA. Normal night and day firing from Monchy throughout the 24 hours. 3rd Division relieved 29th Division in the line and same CRA action and	MM
		2 pm	Took over MG's defence of the line and zones at 2 pm. B/79 detachments withdrawn to wagon line. Casualties: 126023 Lt. HAMIL & Vol Chs (Bty) 84265 Gnr McMAHON	MM
	4		Normal night and day firing	MM
	5		do Casualty: 125366 Gnr McMURDO T. (Bty) Special attention paid to GREEN WORK during hight. Casualty: B11403 Gnr WOOF E.A. Bty (horses)	MM
	6		do	MM
	7		do account of heavy bombardment on left Brigade front. Casualty 149312 Bdr JACKSON W.B. wounded normal night and day firing very quiet throughout 24 hours.	MM
	8	9 am	Harassing fire commenced 500 Rds per 18 Pdr. Bty & 160 per How. Bty when not firing Rate of fire maintained between 5 - 9 am	MM
	9		Harassing fire continued. OP established by B/79 in 02A.d	MM
	10		do Gas bombardment by B/79 on TREE Trench 11pm to 3am	MM
	11		do do 10 pm to 2 am	MM
	12		do Positions of 253 Brigade in H.10 reconnoitred by Adjutant and officer of each Battery with a view to taking over on the 15th.	MM
	13		do Double machine gun emplacement in a shill hole O&C Central observed by B/79. Observed by Capt A Fillingham from O.P. in MONCHY by 2/Lt M.K. ROBINSON from front line (junction of HILL & CANISTER Trenches). Wire laid by 2/Lt R STINSON CASUALTY. 2/Lt R.T.E. HAWNS (wounded)	MM

WAR DIARY
or
INTELLIGENCE SUMMARY.

Army Form C. 2118.

Place	Date	Hour	Summary of Events and Information	Remarks and references to Appendices
MONCHY	June 14		221 rounds R.A. were used. At least 10 direct hits were obtained. Much damage caused. Six Germans were blown into the air. As soon as fire for effect had begun the enemy put a heavy barrage on MONCHY with H.2015 J's as pivot observation. Owing this ineffective to engage our aeroplanes with abnormal intensity. The infantry were cleared from the front line from 2 pm to 6 pm for this shoot.	MM.S.
		7.20 am	HOOK Trench assaulted & captured without artillery barrage. Our Barrage came down at 7.21½ and at 7.25 lifted a LONG Trench was assaulted & rapidly captured. Casualties very slight. Prisoners taken - 2 officers & over 200 o.R.	MM.N
		5.30 pm	Enemy counterattacked but was driven off by our barrage. Parties assembling in BOIS du VERT were seen & successfully engaged by F.O.Os.	MM
	15		Quiet Day. Registration duties. [illegible] [illegible] out. Guns in action 13. Hours in action 6. [illegible] guns main repair.	M/12
	16		at 1.O.M. workshop. 79th Bde 3 guns taken over by 29th Div Artn — [illegible] shuffled. Battery [illegible] hets down to minimum until a slow [illegible] in guns [illegible]. 11 am to 11.15 minutes.	LOT?
ARRAS	17	9 pm 9 am	79th Bde [illegible] guns through line. H.t.p. moved to troops line. ARRAS Battery moved independently to troops line. vacated by 293 Bde at ANZIN. Ammn: [illegible] sent to take over position of 255th Bde R.F.A. at H.E.A.F.U. near POINT DU JOUR	T/P17
ANZIN	18	6 pm 11 pm	79th Bde 18th am from 255th Bn HA at H.E.A.F.U. near POINT DU JOUR. Guns & Hors. Returns posns as follows: A/79 H. 10.C. 40.18 (6 guns) B/79 H. 10. a. 25.05 (5 guns) C/79 H. 10. a. 16.20 (3 guns) D/79 H. 10.C. 20.64 (6 Hors.) on HQ. FAMPOUX — POINT DU JOUR road.	1/417

Place	Date	Hour	Summary of Events and Information	Remarks and references to Appendices
Nex. PONTPOIX	19-		Registration shots being carried out all guns calibrated	WD3
	20.	2.30 AM	D/77 bombard "WASTE" TRENCH for 30 minutes with T.B.s & LTMs still cancels. 1 OR. Lewis (gun). 83652. Bdr WODDING W.	WD2
	21.	9 AM	M/77 came under the orders of OC 50th Div Arty to attack the Left Group of Right Divisional Artillery. XVIII Corps for Tactical purposes.	WD3
		4 PM 16 SPM	Slow bombardment by all Batteries in a area of trenches + shell holes containing Machine Guns. Calibration and registration carried out.	WD3
	22.	10.20 pm	To cooperate with 31st Division on an hyp who carried out minor enterprise D/77 bombarded the SUNKEN RD + dugouts for 20 minutes at I 20 c 77 in Box 3m.	WD3
		11-15 pm	B/77 opened slow trench + trench mortar emplacement bombardment — D/78. Infantry report fire effective in rifting 1m.	
	23.	6.15 AM	B/79 fires 60 RD HE a active trench mortar emplacement. Infantry report.	WD3
	24		Quiet day. awaiting retaliation carried out	
	25.	3.17pm to 3.10 pm	Sunshot bursts of fire on all hilltop by all Batteries at rapid rate of fire. Hostile retaliation slight.	WD3
	26.		Registration for Creeping Barrage on left front of Divisional front. Registration by M/77 for ... destruction of main Granite.	WD3

WAR DIARY
INTELLIGENCE SUMMARY

Army Form C. 2118.

Place	Date	Hour	Summary of Events and Information	Remarks and references to Appendices
New FAMPOUX	27	10 am	Practice Barrage for 15 minutes	W/D 1
		11.30 pm	on my intended operation (which was to capture Sunk Road from pits in no mans land on night of 27-28th June. The enemy) cancelled in favour of occupied pits without much.	
	28	8 am	Registration of WIT TRENCH near GAVRELLE by D/79 matt 18pdrs	W/D 2
		1 pm		
		7.10 pm (2nds)	31st Division attacked CADORNA TRENCH and WOOD ALLEY at GAVRELLE Right Right Divisional Artillery VXIII Corps co-operated with a creeping barrage on XVII Corps front.	
		7.10 to 7.20 pm	18 pdrs fired at rapid rate on enemy barrage line. Reserve opened 50-I lines. D/79 continued barrage on their next on this line until 9.30 pm then resumed normal fire. Operation Attempt. barrage very satisfactory. Objectives gained & about 200 prisoners taken	W/D 3
	29th	12 noon	From 12 noon Harassing fire carried out by 18pdrs in bursts of 5 per minute on CARPET TRENCH (near PLOUVAIN) + this in. kept up throughout 75.	W/D 4
			night in approaches + Battle H.Q. near PLOUVAIN I.15.a. 15. D/79 fired several bursts amongst HANDMILL COPSE	W/D 5
	30th	10 pm	D/79 fires short-Metal Shell for 5 minutes intense on WHALE TRENCH.	
		11.30 pm	" " Lachrymatory shell on the RAILWAY TRIANGLE near PLOUVAIN	
		4.0 am to 4.10 am	Search for by 18pdr + shrapnel. Visibility very low, still very inconvenient round	

W. H. Thompson
Lieut. Adjutant 79 FA. ts

WAR DIARY
or
INTELLIGENCE SUMMARY.

(Erase heading not required.)

Army Form C. 2118.

Appendix — Summary of Events and Information

I Ammunition expended during the month of June
A. 18198   A X 8342   CHEMICAL 1026   "SMOKE" NIL   B X 7285

II Casualties during JUNE
Killed.   Officers. NIL   O.R. NIL
Died of wounds. Officers. 1   O.R. NIL
Wounded.   Officers. ni.   O.R. 6.

III Hostages from sickness.
Officers. 1.   O.R. 16.

IV Casualties & Horses.
Killed, destroyed and died)
                           Total. 3.
Wounded.   NIL
Evacuated to M.V.S.   29 (16 not mange)

W.H. Thompson
Lieut. & Adjutant
for Lieut. Col. Comdg. 79th B.n.R.

WAR DIARY or INTELLIGENCE SUMMARY

79th BRIGADE R.F.A.

JULY 1917

Army Form C. 2118.

Place	Date	Hour	Summary of Events and Information	Remarks and references to Appendices
Near FAMPOUX (on 1% SCALE)	1st		Batteries of 79th Bde R.F.A. in action at following positions:— A/79 H.10.c.4086 (6 guns in action) B/79 H.10.a.2656 (5 guns) C/79 H.10.a.1620 (3 guns) D/79 H.10.c.2864 (6 Hows) H.Qrs at H.8.a.8.4. All wagon lines at ANZIN. (Major C.W.R. TUKE cmdg Bde, in absence of Lt Col L.E. WARREN on leave.)	(illeg)
		11.35 AM	Enemy working party reported I.15 central near PLOUVAIN. This area was shelled by all Batteries at 11.40am intense fire for 5 min.	
	2nd	12.15 AM	All guns in the Bde fired 5 rds gun fire on the same area	
		1 AM	" " " " " " " on WINDMILL CAGE	
		10.47 AM	S.O.S. Rocket reported by Bde O.P. on outcrop from front line of 9th NORTD. FUS. All batteries opened fire at once.	Wd79
		10.54 AM	All reports from front Batteries in the line fire was stopped; all reports gun fire on our front.	
		11.40 PM	An urgent SOS Duke of Wellington (Left Batton) every battery fired 5 rds G.F. on shell-hole in T.8.C.	
	3rd	12.2 AM	FOO reports T.M. are firing from I.2.c.6.1. This was engaged by D/75.	Wd79
		3.45 AM	7 M reports active retaliation by D/79.	
		3.15 AM	18 pdr searched area the shelter not hitting mi- for 5 minutes. Watch the kite at Dawn.	
		12.45 PM	Enemy shell hole at Dawn. Stream was engaged by A/79 OP shooting from I.21.d.2565. in town. Both 7.7 cm guns mggs by A/75 AUTHIE and Silenced.	

Army Form C. 2118.

WAR DIARY
or
INTELLIGENCE SUMMARY.

(Erase heading not required.)

Instructions regarding War Diaries and Intelligence Summaries are contained in F. S. Regs. Part II. and the Staff Manual respectively. Title pages will be prepared in manuscript.

Place	Date	Hour	Summary of Events and Information	Remarks and references to Appendices
PONT POIX	3	2 pm to 8 pm	Deliberate bombardment by D/79 of HAUSA WOOD with South Thereabouts also bombarded by C/77 TRENCH + WINDMILL COPSE. About 30 yds every 4th min back from COST to WINDMILL. No hits on us. Many casualties inflicted on his batteries. Visibility very low. Weather showery.	WD9
	4	10 pm 10.30 PM	18 pdrs & 4.6" Hows carried out a creeping barrage from east street for 10 minutes at an intense rate of fire to find subs lsn.	WD10
	5	4 am	Party of enemy numbering about 40 observed near HAUSA WOOD at I.15.c.5.1 engaged by A/79.	
		1.54 pm	Test S.O.S. A/79 fired	
		4.45 pm	" B/79 "	
		5.22 pm	" C/79 "	
		9.40 pm	6 to 6.15 pm. Enemy shelled battery position heard with 10.5 cm. Hows from BIACHE. Mans one direct hit on C/79. Sgspt pit. Killing 3. O.R. Wounding 1 O.R. A/79 sustained 3 casualties moving ammn from 160 A.Pdr RFA to B/79 position. The casualties below 10 pm & 11 pm on hillside.	
			Killed 52945 Cpl BARRY W.) 9/79 86152 Gnr ANDREWS W.) 76576 Gnr LEE J. } B/79 90747 Gnr NICHOLLS A. Also 3 Horses killed } G.S.W. and 1 mule wounded Band of Fm from enemy shells in B/79 in rear trench when known were working	WMO
			Wounded 9515 Gnr BYTHELL A (9/79) 62057 Dr PHILLIPS T.) B/79 216965 Dr RIPPON N.)	
		10.30 pm	Enemy kept up intermittent fire on a batteries throughout the night.	

WAR DIARY
or
INTELLIGENCE SUMMARY

Army Form C. 2118.

Place	Date	Hour	Summary of Events and Information	Remarks and references to Appendices
Nr. FAMPOUX	6th	Midnight to 3 am	Occasional bursts of artillery in H.10.a. Shells intermittently with 10.5 cm Hows. 4 to 7.7 cm guns. Slackened particularly active all day in trenches and back area	WD
		4 am	Small parties of enemy seen near north edge of HAUSA WOOD and engaged by our 4.5" Hows.	
		10 pm	Throughout the night batteries fired 10.5 cm Hows. and 18 pdr identified to PLOUVAIN - ROEUX Rly.	
	7th	2 am	Enemy reported to be working at T.15.c.23. (ROEUX - PLOUVAIN Rly) and wire entanglements in patrols to our 18 pdr will train of fire on	
		2.55 am	Another working party observed near HAUSA WOOD at I.14.d.8.5 and engaged by D/179	WD
	8th	11.30 pm	Stokes Trench Mortars active at I.8.d.8.0. - persistently annoying our infantry engaged by A/179 with HE. Hostile gun teamed. Wind East 5 (7 calls) Day very quiet.	
	9th	12.10 am	Creeping barrage by all batteries on enemy shell holes in Bar Zone in Bar Zone by an intensive barrage from enemy. Casualties: 1. Or. wounded (Bd. H.)	WD
		1 to 2 minutes intermittent		
		3 pm	Barrage of pins on enemy shell holes in MISTRAIN T. (at OK) 4418 from MISTRAIN T. from all Batteries	WD
	10th	11.35 am 12.30 pm	do do	
			Registration carried out during the night from 10.30 pm to 2.45 pm 2 Rds gun fire were fired by every gun there in the Divisional Artillery in the following targets.	WD
		10.30 pm	RAILWAY TRIANGLE. I.9.d. (near PLOUVAIN Station)	
		10.35 pm	NORM TRENCH I.9.c.	
		10.45 pm	NIBBLE TRENCH "	
		10.50 pm	WEED "	
		11.10	"	

Army Form C. 2118.

WAR DIARY
or
INTELLIGENCE SUMMARY.
(Erase heading not required.)

Instructions regarding War Diaries and Intelligence Summaries are contained in F.S. Regs., Part II. and the Staff Manual respectively. Title pages will be prepared in manuscript.

Place	Date	Hour	Summary of Events and Information	Remarks and references to Appendices
Mon-FAMPOUX	11th	2.0 am.	Bursts of 2 Rds. Gun Fire on following targets at times stated.	
			CLOD TRENCH	
		2.10	Shell holes near our front line	9 pm. T.M. shoots acted by 6th Dorsets arranged by A/79 and Silence. 6/179
		2.15	do	
		2.30 am	WEED TRENCH	
		2.45 am	Tracks from RAILWAY TRIANGLE to ROEUX	
		6.40 pm to 7.30 pm	Enemy shelled our position & H.W.S. lines with 10.5 cm & 15 cm Hows. Replies to H.A.G. & Counter Batteries.	
			New Fire on suspects batteries near 12E4 & FRESNES, (2 Horn byries) D/79	
12th		1.10 am & 2.0 am & 2.50 am	D/79 fired bursts of liked shell on enemy aux. trench to I.9.a. & I.15.a.	W/D
	13th	12-15 am	CLOD TRENCH and S.O.S. received from 7th LINCOLNS. (Blue on an Up.)	
			C/79 & D/79 opens up on their S.O.S. lines for 20 minutes. Enemy attempts to take as an S.O.S. Barrage stops his	W/D
			late cause to an barrage tripwire.	
		12.30 am	A/79 & B/79 fired for 3 minute when reaching on its Right Divisional front. I 20 A.T.B. in front with Thermit	

WAR DIARY
or
INTELLIGENCE SUMMARY.
(Erase heading not required.)

Army Form C. 2118.

Place	Date	Hour	Summary of Events and Information	Remarks and references to Appendices
Pom Poix	13.	4 P.M.	One minute barrage on WIT TRENCH by all B/ties. Timing & burst excellent.	[WD]
		9.12 P.M	Enemy ration party shewed in the Quarry near HANSA WOOD & engaged by A/79.	
		11.15 P.M	Searching fire on enemy shell hole for 2 minutes.	
	14.	2 to 6	During the afternoon B/79 cut wire in front of WART TRENCH many No 106 fuze for two cuttings for the first time. Detonation effect excellent. Registration carried out by B/79 Shot by all batteries.	
		2 to 6 PM	B/79 continued star- shell in front of WART TRENCH to distract enemy attention from pushes of enemy's trench to be raided at 10 P.M.	[WD]
		10 P.M.	Zero Hour for raid carried out by 7th Border Regt. to capture machine gun T.M. & trench dugouts. A/79 firing creeping barrage. B/79 standing Barrage on enemy front line. T.C/79 flank barrage.	
		10.20 P.M	Our infantry back in our own trenches; barrage time successful except:	
		10.45 P.M	Batteries ceased fire. Hit no prisoners taken.	

Army Form C. 2118.

WAR DIARY
or
INTELLIGENCE SUMMARY.
(Erase heading not required.)

Instructions regarding War Diaries and Intelligence Summaries are contained in F. S. Regs., Part II. and the Staff Manual respectively. Title pages will be prepared in manuscript.

Place	Date	Hour	Summary of Events and Information	Remarks and references to Appendices
FAMPOUX	15.		Quiet day. A little repetition.	WD/79
	16.	10.40 am	North B5 (10.5 am) Shelled by flash firing from near GLOSTER WOOD C.26.d.5.8 (engaged by BTC/79 silenced.	WD/79
		3.55 pm	All 18 pdr. fired practice barrage on COST TRENCH for 1 minute.	
		11.5 pm	Immediately. Burst of gun fire all guns + how in approach and support trenches. + DELBAR WOOD. co-operating with 4th Division.	
	17.	2.55 to 3 am	Searching fire on shell holes.	WD/79
		4 pm to 6.30 pm	Successful registration of 4.5" How. by balloon observation on Crew road PLOUVAIN to the target.	
	18.		Harassing fire carried out by D/79 not less 156 rnds on WART TRENCH	WD/79
	19.	3 pm	D/79 fires 105 Rds at T.M. emplacement at T.2.c.8530.	
			D/79 enemy T.M. in WART.	
		10.45 pm	Enemy T.M. active in Railway Cutting and successfully silenced by D/79. Camellia Mill round 1737m, Coffeepot round 7237, Tale GAMBLE P.9. 2097.3 Gr. MORE H (61A.4/79)	WAP
	20.	10.30 pm	Creeping barrage on WART TRENCH by Divisional Artillery. Infantry advance under Barrage (No enemy return). No identification obtained. Barrage (continued until that shell fire are small I. Run ScheRPE)	WD/79
		6-0 Pm to 6.12 Pm	A.5" How	to cement Left Div

WAR DIARY
INTELLIGENCE SUMMARY
(Erase heading not required.)

Army Form C. 2118.

Place	Date	Hour	Summary of Events and Information	Remarks and references to Appendices
New PAMPOUX	21.		Quiet Day, while artillery has active except for concentrated burst of fire by 15 cm on C/178 trenches obtaining direct hit	hMD
		11.40 p.m.	Burst of 2 Shr from the Trojans on RAILWAY at I.14 b 28 at infantry report. effect fair?	
	22	1.15 am	Burst of Shrapnel fire over enemy approaches from PLOUVAIN.	hMD
		6.30 p.m.	D/79 dispersed large enemy party seen near WOTAN TRENCH	
	23	11.0 A.M.	€71.5 P.M. Enemy troops along tracks trapped hitchan.	
		12.15 + 1.20.AM	Burst of fire on enemy network at WART TRENCH	hMD
		7 p.m.	Party of 7 enemy observed near GLOSTER WOOD dispersed by our 18 pdr.	
		9.35pm	D/79 fired a burst on WOTAN TRENCH (I 10 a 7580) when a High - suspected movement always seen at dusk.	
		10.55pm — 11.20 pm + 12.05 AM	18 pdr fired bursts of HE on enemy new work in I 15 d. (near PLOUVAIN)	
	24d		Enemy unusually quiet — A little registration carried out	hMD
		7.20pm	Our 18pdr then fired burst on WOTAN TRENCH	

WAR DIARY
or
INTELLIGENCE SUMMARY.

Army Form C. 2118.

Place	Date	Hour	Summary of Events and Information	Remarks and references to Appendices
FANQUX	24th (cont)	9.50 pm	Burst of fire — movement heard in I.S.d. (PLOUMAN)	W.Q
		10.10 pm	D/79 fired on a suspected R.E. "Dump at BIACHE near station.	
			From 10 pm to midnight an 18 pdr keeping up a ventilating fire on hostile T.M. about the 7th BORDER Rgt. (Regt Bttn. Rifle Bn. Carry.)	
			at Boring & digging operations.	
	25th		Quiet Day. Thunderstorm — visibility bad	Capt C.M.A. HEXTABLE appointed to CRA 13/79 Command B/79. Lieut D.G.A.C. FOREY the 2nd in command of 9/79.
		9.40 pm	18 pdr replied with bursts of fire. Enemy trench & Redm.	
		10.55 pm & 11.20 pm	in 4th Divisional Front — the 4th Div. also covered as	
			similar take on 17th Div. front.	War
		10 pm to 2 am	B/79 also Boud enemy Fire to an enemy party of 7th BORDERS	
	26th	4.45 am	Bombardment by D/79 with Lethel Shell up to 4 guns of D/79 with HE	
			on an enemy patrol south of DELBAR heard to work 4th Division.	
		4.55 am	Batteries ceased firing	
		10 am	Registration of several tryks on 4th Div. Front.	W.H.?
		8.20 pm	Working party observed in WHALE TRENCH Dispersed by D/79	
		10.50 pm to 11.15 pm	Burst of fire on enemy trench 11.20 pm & 11.35 pm. Covering fire trench to 18 pm on working parties of 7th BORDERS.	

WAR DIARY
or
INTELLIGENCE SUMMARY.
(Erase heading not required.)

Army Form C. 2118.

Place	Date	Hour	Summary of Events and Information	Remarks and references to Appendices
Near FAMPOUX.	27th	12 nn to 2 am	5 am. Several small parties of enemy observed near WHALE TRENCH and dispersed by our 18 pdrs.	
		3 pm	Intermittent shelling of our Btys/positions by 7.7cm guns & Fld. skill.	
		3 pm	Corps concentration by all our Hows. for 3 minutes between trenches between MONCHY-LE-PREUX and HERMIN SCARPE. (This was a practice counter-battery shoot in view of a possible hostile attack in M.SUNGKU)	
		5 pm	On minute practice barrage on WHT TRENCH.	
		5.30 pm	Parties of enemy 3 to 4 strong observed coming from BIACHE STATION to ATHALIE TR. An soon as parties had collected together 18 pdr opened fire on them. Casualties seen. Enemy shelled 79 Bn HQ with 10.5 cm gun.	(N.H.?)
	28th	10.30 pm to 3.30 am (28th)	in shorts 10.15 to 11.30 pm. An little 7 mm neutralising harassing shoots fire was kept up by our 18 pdrs	
		4.5 "Hrs	at infantry request.	WHT?
		3 pm	Practice Barrage for 1 minute on WHAT TRENCH.	
		4.67 pm	Registration carried out - nothing particular found on.	
	29th	12.30 am	Zero Hour 2 Companies of the 7th East Yorks Regt. raided WIG and COST TRENCHES, with the Object of obtaining identifications, capturing M.Guns, destroying dugouts, killing Germans. B/79 "Bn.RFA. provided a creeping Barrage & A/79 a standing barrage. D/79 engaged machine guns & T.M.S. 78th + 29th F.A.Bde. + 63rd D.A. also took part in the operation.	(NF)

WAR DIARY
or
INTELLIGENCE SUMMARY.
(Erase heading not required.)

Army Form C. 2118.

Place	Date	Hour	Summary of Events and Information	Remarks and references to Appendices
FRAMPOUX	29.		Retaliatory barrage was kept up at gradually decreasing rates of fire till 1.30 am. when Batteries stopped firing. Rain very frequent. 14 prisoners taken. 1 machine gun & Companies heavy casualties inflicted on the enemy.	
		1.35 am to 3.45 am	harassing fire kept up on all enemy track approaches as a relief in expected opposite to Bonfreux. Enemy's retaliation feeble.	4/17
			Remainder of day quiet – heavy rain.	
	30th	9.30 pm to Midnight	burst of fire on enemy approaches	
		12.45 am. 31/79 snipped burst T.M. at opposite to CROFT TRENCH with good effect		
		9.50 pm	and at my own intervals through night. burst of fire from 18pdrs on enemy track approaches ventilation fire by 4.5" Hows on hostile track mortars	6/17
	31st		Quiet day; visibility low. Immaterialise currents and bursts of fire on enemy approaches and support-trenches.	16/17

W. H. Thompson
Lieut & Adjt.
for Lieut. Col. Comdg. 79th F.A.B.

Army Form C. 2118.

WAR DIARY
or
INTELLIGENCE SUMMARY.
(Erase heading not required.)

79th F.A.B.

APPENDIX of Events and Information — JULY

I. Ammunition expended during the month of JULY.
A. 7410   AX 4681   BX 4255   CHEMICAL 486   SMOKE 73

II. Casualties during JULY.
KILLED   —   Officers NIL   O.R. 4.
DIED OF WOUNDS — Officers NIL   O.R. 1.
WOUNDED   —   Officers NIL   O.R. 4.

III. Wastage from Sickness: Officers NIL   O.R. 7.

IV. Casualties to Horses } Killed 3.
and Mules } Died 1.
Evacuated to M.V.S. 80.

W.H. Thompson.
Lieut.
for Lieut. Col. Comdg. 79th F.A.B.

Army Form C. 2118.

WAR DIARY
INTELLIGENCE SUMMARY.
(Erase heading not required.)

79th F.A 73.   AUGUST 1917.   Vol 25

Place	Date	Hour	Summary of Events and Information	Remarks and references to Appendices
Near ROMPOUX	1.		Batteries of 79th Bde in action at following position. (Map 51.B.N.W.)	
			A/79. H.10.c.71.46.	
			B/79. H.10.c.56.65. Bde. H.qrs. at H.8.a.80.30.	
			C/79. H.10.c.45.84.	
			D/79. H.10.c.39.37. Bde.Hqrs. at ANZIN.	7/Lt. R.M. WALKER 8/39 35th D.A. posts to 51st D.A. WAR ?
	12.40 am.	Burst of fire from all guns on enemys approaches.	2/Lt. J. NEWMAN-BUTLER posts to 55th D.A.
	5 pm	One minute barrage by all 18 pdrs on WIG TRENCH.	
			6.2 pm to 8.7 pm a light barrage in retaliation was put on our supports	
2.	2 pm	One minute barrage on WART TRENCH	
		Reconnaissance by Adjutant to front O.P. from which to observe hostile barrage on WART. WAR?	
	11.15 pm to 11.50 pm Harassing bombardment of enemy approaches and support.	
			Trenches in bursts of fire at irregular intervals.	
3.	10.35 pm and again at 10.45 pm a one minute barrage was put down on CRUST	WAR?
			and CUB Trenches	
4.	4 PM Working party observed and engaged by our 18 pdrs at T 14 c 39. Casualties	WAR
			inflicted appeared to be 2 killed and 13 wounded.	
	3.10 pm. Active F.M. Schemes for harassing fire from our 18 pdrs.	
			Normal night firing on enemy approaches.	

WAR DIARY
or
INTELLIGENCE SUMMARY.

(Erase heading not required.)

Army Form C. 2118.

Place	Date	Hour	Summary of Events and Information	Remarks and references to Appendices
NEW FAMPOUX	5.		Day quiet: a little registration carried out. During the day at intervals enemy were seen moving trucks leading to saw-mill works (at I 2 & 7.2) several being recognised as officers; and men with white bands on their fore caps (probably WURTEMBURGERS). An O.P. suspected was reported by Lt. GREVILLE. (Chaunin Officer with 8th S. Staff[r].) Close to the trench mentioned.	
		10.35 p.m.	Fire was opened by 18/79 on this place on officers, good opportunity offered. 2/ 7th BORDER Regt. (Right Battn.) fired on our fighting patrol under cover of an barrage between our lines CRUST & CUB. a team of our scouts shell holes with hand strong men. Party held up by m.m and a machine gun. 11.5 pm All fell ceased. Have night training in trench & approach.	WD
	6.	2 am	For 3 minutes burst of explosive fire by 8 18pdrs & 4 Hows to assist 4th Division Artillery on front in the SCARPE VALLEY.	
		10.55 am	A T.M reported firing on CUPID TRENCH from the Railway Cutting, engaged and trench[man] silenced by our 18 pdrs.	
		3 Pm.	Movement in repeated in the enemy support line (I 8 c 4590). The party were	

WAR DIARY
INTELLIGENCE SUMMARY

Army Form C. 2118.

Place	Date	Hour	Summary of Events and Information	Remarks and references to Appendices
Near PAMPOUX	7	11.50 p.m	Patrol of 1 Officer and 2 Privates 18th & 16th Tch Division Officer and Rifle Bn report enemy working parties in NO MANS LAND 18 Pdrs put up a shoot of five on places reported: result not known.	Tops
	7.	7.9 am	T.M at SHERWOOD HAUSA WOOD fired on by 4.5" How. and silenced for several hours. A Suspected M.G. emplacement in COPSE trench (I.20.b.70.65) has [Couply?] registered by D/79 with observation from trench. COLOMBO (I.20.a.30.50) Cpy. shot lit on Mound on top of concrete loophole. Division Officer reports that the enemy were busy today in a line behind [illegible] in front of CREST everywhere ought to work new trench. Parties of the enemy shown from Bar O.P. were at times engaged by our 18 Pdr with good results. Mpls firing on enemy approaches and working parties T.M.S. Quiet day.	TMS
	F.	1.30 am to 7.33 am B/79 searched HAUSA WOOD to assist the 4th Divisional Artillery Mpls firing: heads of Pri on breaks and approach to catch enemy working.			TMS

T2134. Wt. W708—776. 500000. 4/15. Sir J.C. & S.

WAR DIARY
INTELLIGENCE SUMMARY
(Erase heading not required.)

Army Form C. 2118.

Place	Date	Hour	Summary of Events and Information	Remarks and references to Appendices
Mt FAMPOUX	9th	5 pm	Our working party just south of SQUARE WOOD fired on and dispersed by an 18 pdrs. Comrade movement was reported in trenches seen by the T.O.D	WD
	16th		Several hostile planes were engaged and dispersed during the afternoon. Quiet Day.	WD
	11th	10.30 pm to midnight	Irregular bursts of fire on back area and enemy approaches.	
		7 am	F.O.O. reports armoured train movement behind VITRY coming from and going in a northerly direction.	
	12th	9 pm to midnight	Hostile T.M.s active in our frontline engaged by D/79. Lieut E. GILDON brought Mg from in trench to catch relief. VI Corps Heavy Artillery.	WD
		9.50 pm and 10.50 pm	A few parties of enemy observed and engaged by an 18 pdrs. 18 pdr fired burst on RAILWAY CUTTING near WARD MILL COPSE & also at 10.25 pm on enemy wiremark.	WD
	13th		A/15 each burst of gun enemy retaliates with short bursts of fire on batteries. Hostile T.M.s engaged caused him many tonight. Day quiet.	
		2 pm to 2.30 pm	A/79 & B/79 provided covering fire for an Trench Mortar by from Infantry at irregular intervals in HARSA NITED to hinder Herring	

3 Infantry Officers attached for 10 days instruction { Capt F.R. MILLIGAN (7th Vols. Flanders), Capt X.S. RIDGE (12th Manchester), Lieut S.J. WEEDHAM M.C. 3/4 R.W. Kents

Army Form C. 2118.

WAR DIARY
or
INTELLIGENCE SUMMARY.
(Erase heading not required.)

Instructions regarding War Diaries and Intelligence Summaries are contained in F. S. Regs., Part II. and the Staff Manual respectively. Title pages will be prepared in manuscript.

Place	Date	Hour	Summary of Events and Information	Remarks and references to Appendices
Nr FAMPOUX	14th	5:20 pm	A party of enemy consisting of 3 Men and 12 men (seen) near CANDY TR. I 14 a 9.5.8. Division in the party and apparently working out line of trench on dugouts. B/173 brigade target dispersed the party knocking 1 officer.	—/M/2
		5 pm to 6 pm	187pdr howitzer covering fire for our T.M.a During the night lewis [?] T.M. + Rifles fire on 4.8 Hour. Places fit on 4.8 Hour also covered out a CHEMICAL shell bombardment of WINE an ATTILLE trenches	
	15th	2.20 pm	Enemy working parties observed at I.8.c.5.7.5 and engaged by our 18pdrs and dispersed.	
		4.15 pm	Another enemy working party dispersed by our 18pdr.	1/M/2
		2 pm to 3 pm	our 18pdrs provided covering fire for our T.M.'s shooting on CREST.	Shell by letter 2/Lieut A. J. HUBBERT drowned at BOULOGNE recently [?]
	16"	11.10am to 11.25 am & 3.46 am	Our Heavy guns neutralized enemy T.M. 2 Lording knots fires on dugouts during night by our 18pdrs.	
		3.40 am to 4.30 am	T.M. + rear Railway Cutting annihilated by 18pdrs.	
		4.30 am	Enemy defensive barrage enemy fired on No Man's Land immediately engaged + dispersed by our 18 pdrs	
		3.5pm	Enemy working party near PLOUVAIN (I.5.d.5.6) known on and turn + cover supper annihilated by our 18pdr.	M/2
		3.37pm	Enemy working party dispersed in same locality dispersed by our 18pdr. Again reorganize reinforcements arrived.	
		10 pm	Bombardment of enemy lines carrying line in all enemy approach at Ayette front by 9", 6", Enemy retaliation on Battery positions with H.E. & Hun gas.	

WAR DIARY
or
INTELLIGENCE SUMMARY

(Erase heading not required.)

Place	Date	Hour	Summary of Events and Information	Remarks and references to Appendices
Nr FAMPOUX	17th		Work of reconstructing gun pits began to allow of fire extending from GAVRELLE CEMETERY down to SANDPIT (I 27 d) Sunday river SCARPE. Small parties of enemy seen on bank. They at intervals by our 18 pdrs. Harassing fire continued during day on work done by all enemy parties.	WD1
	18th	1 am	18 pdrs (J 30 R+5 Fox) on enemy return harassing fire by all 18 pdrs. Intense approach in view suspected enemy relief in the CHEMICAL CO. WORKS SECTOR.	WD2
		3.15 pm	Dispersed a GREENLAND HILL working party on an Enemy near Railway much interrupted shelter. Night quiet.	
	19th		Registration of 4.5" Hows on three targets by Balloon and shelter in 16 pdr. Howrs by aeroplane registration. Registration of T.M. dispersed. 12.35 pm and 6/7 am an 18 pdr. dispersed enemy. 10 am to 20.30 am by T.M.s shot built up fire on HAUSA WOOD and on T.M. Enemy O.P.s. Night quiet.	WD3
	20th		Worked further any tgts by an 18 pdr. Enemy fire for and T.M's shelter on CRUST on proven by A + B/79 Craving from 11.30 am to 12 noon and from 1 pm to 1.35 pm. 15 pm L.T.M. work on hostile Stunning and Shelter at troops in line AN 2 IN in kind. Skital hown and enemy return hurrassing return of attacks. Mortars begun. Newburlogus fire on T.M in. at night by our 18 pdr. fire S Mrws	WD4

WAR DIARY
INTELLIGENCE SUMMARY

Army Form C. 2118.

Place	Date	Hour	Summary of Events and Information	Remarks and references to Appendices
Near FAMPOUX	21st		Quiet day.	
	22nd	10.15pm	Lt. Col. Charles Ferguson, Comdg. XVII Corps visited Battery/Position. Some retaliation carried out and retaliation opened on hostile T.M. From midnight to 12.30 a.m. 6 bursts of fire from all 18pdrs was directed on enemy new work and support trenches.	No.47
	23rd	2.15am	Enemy firing fairly numerous but slightly. Retaliatory rounds on CRUST Trenches, followed by A/79. Bombardment with gas shell amongst A/79 15 pm on hostile guns & bombardment area. Night quiet.	No.49
		5 pm	Searchers for hun B/79 an enemy new trench. A/79 sent up to engage any movement seen. B/79 bombarded CRUST and CANDY Trenches. Cancelled owing to no movement seen. Gas shell bombardment by all 4.5" How. Medium Trench T.M.'s 30 minutes. CLOD, CLIFF, with intense searching fire. CAN. COW. CLIFF CLAY. Cooperated afterwards on Railway cutting. Uprika! all enemy movement seen.	No.49
	24th	10pm to 10.8 pm 10.55pm	Gas shell harassing fire continued up to 11.30 pm. Some registration carried out. Quiet day. Night. 50th Inf. Bde relieved 52nd Bde	No.A.?
	25th	9.15pm and 11.6.0pm 3-15a to 4.30am	T.M. active in THIS WOOD, silenced by our 4.5" How. 9 bursts of fire from all 18pdrs on enemy trench and support trenches. Infantry & consolidated shelters. Day quiet.	No.A.?

WAR DIARY
INTELLIGENCE SUMMARY

Army Form C. 2118.

Place	Date	Hour	Summary of Events and Information	Remarks and references to Appendices
Near FAMPOUX	26th		Day quiet: a few small parties of enemy engaged by our 18 pdr with effect.	W/02
	27th	2.am - 2.15am - 2.40am - 2.50am - bursts of 2 rds fire from Cheyenne Trench at 18pdr on enemy trench near WASH TRENCH & FRECKENHAM.		W/02
			Two enemy parties engaged by 87 & our 18pdr. Weather very stormy. Enemy abnormally low: visibility very bad.	
		10pm to 11pm	Burst of fire from 18 pdr on enemy trench.	W/02
	28th	6.30am	Large party of enemy seen in WATTLE TRENCH engaged by B/95 with shrapnel. Weather very stormy: accurate shooting impossible.	W/03
	29th		Several parties of the enemy in the open near WATTLE TRENCH seen very effectively engaged by 18 pdr. Weather very stormy. Harassing fire all night.	W/02
	30th	3.30pm	Attack by him Bombardment of CLOD + CONVOY Trenches by all batteries in co-operation with 2" T STM Mortars of 50th Division Bde. 30 T.R.D. fired. Enemy retaliated by a Non-minnenwerfer bombardment. But damage to the CONVOY. Bde quiet. No casualties. Heavy trench mortar barrage on the whole Bn S from enemy trench.	W/02
	31st	10 pm to 10.15pm	Burst of fire by all 18pdr.	
		2.40am & 2.45am & 2.57 am	Bursts of shrapnel & bursts of fire. Enemy very quiet. 16 harass enemy all night.	W/09
			A few enemy working parties engaged.	
Arrivisse on August 28th	3 officers McKenzie (9th Duke of Wellington's) TO A/79. Capt. Hall (6th R.F.A.) to B/79. Capt. Redfern (7th E. Yorks) to D/79.		for 14 days instruction.	

W. A. Thompson Capt. R.F.A. T/Adjt
for Lieut Col Comdg 79th F.A.B.

WAR DIARY
INTELLIGENCE SUMMARY

79th Bde RFA   AUGUST 1917

—APPENDIX—

Hour	Summary of Events and Information	Remarks and references to Appendices
I	Ammunition expended during month of AUGUST: A. 6035 AX. 3935. BX 2256 CHEMICAL 337. SMOKE 46.	
II	Casualties during AUGUST: KILLED — Officers NIL O.R. NIL WOUNDED — Officers NIL O.R. NIL (Accidentally drowned at BOULOGNE when returning from leave to ENGLAND 1 Officer. 2/Lt. A.J. HIBBERT. 3/7/9.)	
III	Wastage from Sickness: Officers NIL. O.R. 11.	
IV	Casualties to Horses & Mules: KILLED NIL DESTROYED or DIED 2 horses EVACUATED to M.V.S. 16. horses	

W.H. Thompson
Capt RFA
Adjutant 79th FAB

ᶠ Lieut Col. Comdg 79 FAB

Army Form C. 2118.

WAR DIARY
or INTELLIGENCE SUMMARY

79th F.A.B.   SEPTEMBER 1917

Vol 26

Place	Date	Hour	Summary of Events and Information	Remarks and references to Appendices
Near FAMPOUX	1st	4.35 am	D/79 fired on Hostile T. Mortar at infantry report. Since Enemy has withdrawn most of his 15 cm and 10.5 cm Hostile Batteries from the Sector behind GAVRELLE and ROEUX, the has been intermittently shelling our forward area batteries whilst our active intermittently in annihilation and support fire from dusk to dawn. 79th Bde occupies the same positions as last month as follows :— A/79 H.10.c.71.46. B/79 H.10.c.56.65. C/79 H.10.c.45.84. D/79 H.10.c.29.37. 79th Bde R.F.A. covering the 50th Inf. Bde in CHEMICAL WORKS SECTOR. Bn H.Q. at H.8.a.8.3.3. Transom Lines at ANZIN. The work of constructing new standings with new cover & erection of huts being carried on with all possible neutralising fire at intervals on hostile T.M's by our Hows.	$\frac{V \cdot 4/9}{}$
	2nd	10 pm to 12.45 am	Enemy Gun shell (bombardment with littles) shell by D/79 on Battn Hqrs near PLOUVAIN in NEED TRENCH. Enemy did not retaliate	$\frac{U \cdot 4/9}{}$
		1.45 pm	Working parts seen in PLOUVAIN apparently enemy also working. Road on their front.	
	3rd	4.40 am	D/79 neutralise hostile T.M. at infantry report. G.O.C. R.A. 3rd Army (General Lecky) visits the Battery position during the morning. Enemy working parties engaged at same ref. point by our 18 pdrs. Hostile Trench Mortar engaged during the night.	$\frac{W \cdot 4/9}{}$

Army Form C. 2118.

WAR DIARY
or
INTELLIGENCE SUMMARY.
(Erase heading not required.)

Instructions regarding War Diaries and Intelligence
Summaries are contained in F. S. Regs. Part II.
and the Staff Manual respectively. Title pages
will be prepared in manuscript.

Place	Date	Hour	Summary of Events and Information	Remarks and references to Appendices
Nr PAMPOUX	4.		Usual hostile Trench Mortar activity during the early morning, & inactivity during the day 4.5 hours + 18 pdr.	
		10.30 pm	Quietroy ruented very low pents enemy when hostile billows aroused into increased hostile artillery activity. 3 pm. Hostile working party begun. 17# Divisional Artillery fired 2 pts fire from all 18 pdrs on enemy front.	WD
		11.0 + 11.15 pm	line along Trenks 5.7 pm in support Trenkh S.W of PLOUVAIN.	
		11.25 pm	Burst of fire on enemy Track CANDY & Cottar PIT.	WD
		5.		Several enemy Batteries engaged + dispersed by our 18pdrs. Destruction shoots by 6.5 in How Bty with an CANDY Battery known.	WD
		6. 10.30 am	No casualties. Our Guns Not present at our action for 36 hours. Hostile retaliation from self damages & inst instantaneous fuges. N147 prematuere of C/79. Ruts damages & levels by RE.	WD
	7.	6 pm 6.45 pm 6 pm	Battalion & immediately engaged by Heavy Artillery. Hostile hints of 2.2 em near PLOUVAIN STATION dispersed by our 18pdr. 2 men killed & 4 men injured. Thurst E.A.H. GRYLLS B/79 appointed Our recent bump by all 18pdr on KART TRENCH. Enemy retaliates vigorously with mud motors.	WD
	8.		Visibility very bad all O.G. 2nd Lieut (a/Capt) A. FILLINGHAM (D/79) appointed to command D/79 5th Bde RFA 15th Division. Lieut E.T.D. BURTON (D/79) appointed 2nd in command g D/79 5th Bde RFA.	WD

Army Form C. 2118.

WAR DIARY
or
INTELLIGENCE SUMMARY.
(Erase heading not required.)

Place	Date	Hour	Summary of Events and Information	Remarks and references to Appendices
New FAMPOUX	8th continued	6 pm to 6.35 pm	Concentrated bombardment by our 18 pdrs & 4.5in Hows in Co-operation with Heavy Arthy & T.M. on enemy lines WINDMILL COPSE and PROVAIN windmill. 2/Lieut. PATTERSON observed from a flank O.P. on 4th Division front in addition to Bn F.O.O. from Bn. O.P.	W.O.?
	10 pm (Zero)	Raid on HART & HOPE TRENCHES by 12th Munchester Regt. (52nd Bde) with Object of causing destruction & destroying T.M.'s Machine guns and dugouts. 9 Officers & 240 O.R. Munchesters and 1 Officer & 15. O.R. 93rd Fd Coy R.E. took part in raid. Raid most successful. Barrage reported excellent. 79th Bn R.F.A. horsed the enemy's barrage. But so far no evidence available, the first wave of attack closed into within 30 from where 20 Officer and O.R. Munchesters together, working party in WORM TRENCH dispersed by an 18 pdr. 3/79 Bey deter mustered from CANDY to CHALK PIT by balloon burst & put on enemy approach, burning the night. 18 pdrs in several supports enemy. Relief in the GREENLAND HILL Sector.	W.O.?
	9th 9 pm			
	10th 4.30pm 10.30 & 11.30pm	Working party of 4 hours hurried on COST TRENCH and new track from CANDY to the CHALK PIT. 4 & 11.30 pm 18 pdr puts bursts in WEED TRENCH dispersed by our 18 pdr. Enemy annoying machine gun fire on COST TRENCH and new track from CANDY Day quiet.	W.O.?
	11th	4.15 & 4.45 pm about 11 AM.	Enemy working parties in COST engaged & dispersed our 18 pdrs. Night quiet.	T.M.Q.

A.5834 W—W4973/M687 750,000 8/16 D.D. & L. Ltd. Forms/C.2118/13.

Army Form C. 2118.

WAR DIARY
or
INTELLIGENCE SUMMARY.
(Erase heading not required.)

Instructions regarding War Diaries and Intelligence Summaries are contained in F. S. Regs., Part II. and the Staff Manual respectively. Title pages will be prepared in manuscript.

Place	Date	Hour	Summary of Events and Information	Remarks and references to Appendices
Neuville Vitasse	12.		Hostile Artillery was quiet although our Batteries did much registration. Think Trench Mortars very active.	
		4.45-5.30pm	Enemy put down a T.M's barrage on our front line in the T.M's exploits covering fire for an T.M's barrage on our supposed T.P.O. nothing public [illegible] supposed down afterwards.	
	13.	11.45am	Our 9" mortars opened down on hostile Hts. A.A.9 pm in an function	
		12.30pm	Enemy replied putting heavy repeatedly on CRAB WHIP TRENCH.	
		3.45pm	[illegible] parties in same place [illegible] Bulgarian.	
	14.	Am 1pm	[illegible] fired during the morning from T.M's	
		2 pm	broken parts in TREES TREES TRENCH [illegible] by our 13 pdr.	
		4.5pm	Moving [illegible] Routes including 2 [illegible] out picked [illegible] apparently on Shoulders [illegible] and [illegible] from to our in TREES TRENCH [illegible]	
			[illegible] high velocity shells landing [illegible] to [illegible] more increased. One Mills Rampart broken away.	
			[illegible] T.M. trajectory (I.B.6 7095) known by R/79	
			into 80 hrs. HE. [illegible] met-will [illegible] [illegible]	
			During afternoon were thrown into the air.	
	15.		Several working parties fired on and dispersed during the day. Enemy carried [illegible]	
		8 pm	The end of GREENLAND HILL except by one Shrapnel Shower carries fired	
	16.	9 am	A our minute practice barrage was put down on CRUST TRENCH which [illegible] Enemy parties in the [illegible] on night of 15th-16th by the 51st Brigade. 2/Lieut. R. Simson [illegible] Officer with the Right Bn. (Capt. M. Rosedew Reigate 9th B.) was [illegible] [illegible] on practice [illegible] when trying to put —	

WAR DIARY or INTELLIGENCE SUMMARY

Army Form C. 2118.

Place	Date	Hour	Summary of Events and Information	Remarks and references to Appendices
Near FAMPOUX	16th		Iam: Flank Guards in also attacked by 2/Lieut N.A. MURGATROYD from nervous hour in ROEUX. Enemy shots a little Barrage reported at M.30 then put preparatory barrage at M.30 then. 17th Div. Arty Operation Order No 139. A Barrage kept in short bursts from front line it although on to which shows the direction towards enemy front line, 10 clear to new his to breaking difficulties any to carry back repetitions front line + the offrents. Murgatroyd	
	9 hour	ZERO HOUR. Party of 4 Officers + 68 O.R. of 10th SHERWOOD FORESTERS. (51st Bde.) attacked CRUST TRENCH. (under A.B on which trench) Zero to 3min +1 A/79 T B/79 previous barrage on CRUST TRENCH. 3min to 6min +2 C/D/75 Y.S. T B 3min + 2. D/79 then on objects target. 6min + 2 to 16min +15 Took barrage lifted rate 3min + 15 per minute 16min + 2 to... came back in an hour. enemy shells. many German balls. Barrage reports very accurate and known shape. 1 captured + T.M 2 improvement known up (52nd Bde) This raid attracted enemy attention to the part of R.L line every 1 captured. we had no casualties at night. from WIT TRENCH this we had no casualties at night.	
	12 MIDNIGHT	Raid on WIT TRENCH by 12th MANCHESTER REGT. in zero. enemy barrage reported by 78th & 79th Brigades RFA. (63rd Div Arty also co-operated.) Barrage reports very successful. Lt Mumm late many killed) + 6 dry not known about successful. Lt Mumm. Out 2 M.Gs. captures, our losses slight.	[C/HQ]

A.5834. Wt. W4973/M687. 750,000. 8/16 D.D. & L. Ltd. Forms/C.2118/13.

Army Form C. 2118.

WAR DIARY
or
INTELLIGENCE SUMMARY.
(Erase heading not required.)

Instructions regarding War Diaries and Intelligence Summaries are contained in F. S. Regs., Part II. and the Staff Manual respectively. Title pages will be prepared in manuscript.

Place	Date	Hour	Summary of Events and Information	Remarks and references to Appendices
New Farm Roeux	17th		Day quiet. The usual small working parties engaged in defence by an 18 pdr. & hostile T.M's. retaliated.	
	18th		Several working parties engaged (during day). Hostile T.M's (retaliatory) active on night of 18-19 inst. Engaged hostile T.M's with 18 pdr's & with H.E. Burst of fire from our 18 pdrs silenced an 18 pdr with H.E. No enemy attacks appeared.	
	19th		Quiet 24 hours. A few small working parties dispersed.	
	20th		do do do Trench mortars.	
			Troublesome during the night. Silenced by 18 pdrs with HE.	
	21st		Day quiet. A few small working parties dispersed.	
	22	2 am	3 minute bursts of lethal shell by do Howrs on bank in I 15 c 3 d	
	23	3.15am	Day quiet. Burst of fire on trucks etc extricating lorry and upon	
	24	4 am	Heavy enemy barrage (artillery and T M's) on front line & support's from ROEUX to the Railway.	
		4.35	We opened up protective barrage. About 60 of the enemy were	
		4.40	SOS, Coy HQrs received and acted on. They were discovered by a patrol and dispersed by MG's the barrage at took one prisoner and cloud opp on no mans land during the day & stopped true too on on to attack TM positions in conjunction with 6"	

Army Form C. 2118.

WAR DIARY
or
INTELLIGENCE SUMMARY.
(Erase heading not required.)

Place	Date	Hour	Summary of Events and Information	Remarks and references to Appendices
FAMPOUX	Sept. 25. 1917		In the line - 182nd Bde on the right, 183rd Bde (61st Div) on the left, 184th Bde in reserve. Line taken over by 61st Div. midnight 24/5 Sept. Day quiet.	
	26	9 pm.	One section of A B C & D Batteries relieved by 307th Bde R.F.A. (61st Div). Day quiet. A further section relieved by 307th Bde at 9 pm.	
	27	9 pm.	Trench mortars very troublesome in early morning from 8 - 9.30 am. Relief complete. Defence of line passed to 307th Bde.	
ANZIN ST AUBIN	28.		Brigade at Wagon Lines resting refitting	
	29		do	
	30		do	

Lewarne
Lt. Col. Cmdg
79th Bde R.F.A.

Army Form C. 2118.

WAR DIARY
or
INTELLIGENCE SUMMARY.

(Erase heading not required.)

79th F.A.B. APPENDIX

Summary of Events and Information September 1917

I	Ammunition Expended September 1917
	3576 A 3934 PX 2367 BX Chemical 104.
II	Casualties during August.
	KILLED Officers NIL OR NIL
	WOUNDED Officers NIL OR 11
III	Wastage from Sickness
	Officers NIL OR 11
IV	Casualties to horses + mules
	KILLED NIL
	EVACUATED 12 horses
	DIED 1 horse

Sturewen Lt. Col. Comdg.
79th Bde R.F.A.

Raid on CRUST TRENCH 9 pm 16" Sept/17
by 10th SHERWOODS & 8. R.E.

Raid on WIT TRENCH. 16th–17th Sept. 1917
by 12th Manchester Regt. 52nd Bde.
and 1 Officer and 15 OR of 93rd Field Coy RE

WTT TRENCH RAID.

WAR DIARY
INTELLIGENCE SUMMARY

79th FAB ~~September~~ October 1917

Vol 27

Army Form C. 2118.

Place	Date	Hour	Summary of Events and Information	Remarks and references to Appendices
ANZIN – ST. AUBIN.	1		Brigade resting & refitting. Orders received to leave Third Army at night & join the Fifth Army. Preparations to entrain.	
Mt. ARENT.	2		HQrs entrained at ARRAS with Mr. Lukin 17th DAC to CASSEL station	A/79
		2 AM	to 11 AM. Batteries entrained at various times the following	B/79
		3 AM	arrived CASSEL at 3 AM. 2nd inst.	C/79
			Entrained at CASSEL HQrs and batteries proceeded independently by WEMARS – CAPPEL and NORDPEENE.	
			Route march to HERZEELE	
			HQrs arrived billets near HERZEELE at 6 PM.	D/79
			A/79 at 9 PM, B & C/79 entrained during the night. D/79 arrived	
	3	8 AM	at 12 noon on the 3rd.	
			Bde Cmdr & B.Cs proceeded by motor lorry to reconnoitre battery	
			positions N.E. of YPRES near RUITERN, LANGEMARCK	E/79
Near PROVEN.		1.30 PM	Bde moved to 'W' Camp, 3 miles N. of POPERINGHE, and arrived in the HULSEREKEN	
	4		Further reconnaissance during the day. Battery positions.	
			Preparations during the day.	
	5		All echelon 'A' moving into taken up gun positions during the night. Battery positions as follows:	
			A/79 C.4.a.40.80	
			B/79 C.4.a.35.55	
			C/79 C.4.a.60.75 to 70.80 } Near
			D/79 C.4.a.10.75 } LANGEMARCK
			Bde HQrs established at ADELPHI HOUSE C.3.B.15.70 (2nd stand by 78 K Bde HQrs)
			9/79 moved to Gun DOVER F. 9/29.	

Capacity Gun DOVER F. 9/29 mounted GunN.

WAR DIARY or INTELLIGENCE SUMMARY

Army Form C. 2118.

Place	Date	Hour	Summary of Events and Information	Remarks and references to Appendices
ELVERDINGHE	6.		Horse Lines moved to ELVERDINGHE. Batteries (Reputed) now subject-candidates of Bdes vacated post. 78 & 79 the Divl RFA Brigades forming the Right Group of 15 RFA. carried to 12" Bde. 4th Division. H. Rght Group worker under the command of Bde Cdr. A.G. ARBUTHNOT. CMG DSO.	WD1
	(1x 7th Day)		Report this Well Patterns completed training with reconnaissance, OPs etc.	WD2
			Casualties wounded Sergt STEPHENSON. J. C/73 GARRETT. H. 6/10/17 Gnr LAFTON. E. G/ WHITTINGHAM. S.	
	8.		Area bombardments carried out by all Batteries from 6.25 am to 8.55 pm. air from 2 to 2.3 am.	WD3
			Casualties wounded. Gnr BROWN W. A/73 Bdr WADDELL. S. G. C/73 7/10/17 Gnr CURTISPATCH T. C/73	
	9. (2 am) 5.20 Am Zero Hour		The XIV Corps & the XVIII Corps attacked. The former Known to 4th Divl artillery. Th 12th Div centre the groups driving in watering of 79 + 78 Bde RFA supported the Right Division (right shoulder) 78 Bde not C/79 Battery moving the Curtury trainage A & D/73 moved the strong trainage C & D/78 + M B/79 + B/79 Did & attached with the 3th Inf Bde, 10th Bde in support + M B/79 to the attack was carried out in 3 trainages, to each in reserve	
			congratulated all batteries moved company trainage Effects an intentionally an incident	
			Divn Officers attached Capt. D.G. B.C. PARRY. (C/78.) FOO with the attacking Bde: Tau R. & G. W. Lt.	(WD)
			was Lieut G.S. WALKER. (B/73) who became carried on forward. "The finding to the known apr. Casualty wounded. Gnr TAYLOR G. G/73 information	

WAR DIARY
or
INTELLIGENCE SUMMARY.

Army Form C. 2118.

Place	Date	Hour	Summary of Events and Information	Remarks and references to Appendices
Near LANGEMARCK			[handwritten entries largely illegible]	
			Grand By of 17th Division but all objectives had the night of 7th to 8th largely by 17th Div. Infy to POELCAPELLE Brewery [...] HELLES HOUSE and POELCAPELLE Brewery [...] British left [...] coping with [...] barrage [...] holding ground [...] infantry turn and barrage too fast [...] somewhere returning thus.	MR2
	10	11:45 p.m.	On enemy stf [...] near [...] before [...] stf and all [...] approached [illegible] fire. No counterattack in the [...] forward [...] [...] [...] TFn [...] enemy's counter [...] kept up [...] attacks [...] Hunt C.D. MORGAN M.C. 173 wounded Bn Comd. G. 13/2 [...]	MR2 / MR2
	11		Do.	
	12		The attacks of the 9th & 11th were resumed for the capture of [...] Trial Objectives on the morning of the 12th Corps Front. XIV Corps attacked at 5:25 a.m. not at 3:00 a.m. as right. 17 Div on Centre	Casualties: Wounded: Lt Col MORGAN 1/2/9/13 92 DAUSSPORT A. 979
		5:25 a.m.	and [...] Div on left. The 17th Div (XIV Corps) attacked with 70 Bde and 1 Bn attached and 4th Div front the enemy barrage [...] right & well dn? 2 gun batteries 700 [...] by HELLES HOUSE and REQUETTE FARM 17th Div - Cannot tell [...] 700 casualties [...] that kept the [...] vehicle and potatoes barrage (?) [illegible]	On Staff of POELCAPELLE: Gunners Tim MILLS E.W. 9/13 Cpl SMITH R. 9/13 MR2

WAR DIARY
INTELLIGENCE SUMMARY.

79 FA/B

Army Form C. 2118.

Place	Date	Hour	Summary of Events and Information	Remarks and references to Appendices
NEW LANGEMARCK	13	3 p.m.	The Regiment A/C/79 withdrew to the Wagon Lines for 96 hours rest. A + B/79 took over the Defences of the Box front.	W/2
	14.	8 a.m.	Harassing fire carried out all night. No enemy approach. The 70th & 71st Bde R.F.A. relieved the Right Artillery Group under command of B.G. HRA. We took over Gp HQ at BOIS AVELETTE	A/79
	15		A little harassing fire carried out by night. Counterbattery kept up in vicinity of our Batteries.	
	16.			Casualties: Killed Gnr BINNS C. C/79 Wounded D. Gps (ret duty) Gnr COLLINSON E. A/79 Br CONNOR 18/5 COCKAYNE M.J. Major WITH GUSSIE MC cmdg A/79 Gr LONSDALE J. (B/79) Lieut C.B. REED A/79 Gr SNELL A. B/79 Gr LAWTON E M4/79 Gr WILSON W H D/79 Gr FOSTER N C/79 Gr WALKER HH D/79
			Note 10.5 I.S.F. AFE returning our Grr Major Gps ATE returning our "B/79" Wounded (by bombs at WL) Gnr LAWTON E m4/79	WO/2
	17.	8 a.m.	70th & 71st "B" Bdes moved to LH Group of the Regiment. Covering 103rd Bde of the 35th Division G.O.C.R.A 17th Div XIV Corps front changed from a 3 divisional to a 2 divisional front.	
		3 p.m.	A/79 Howitzer returned to position "C/79 took over the Gun 1/8/79 18 guns in action. One 4.5 How Drvmgs by Shellfire Casualties held for been broken up - taken to 10 mins. broken up.	W/2
	18.		Abnormal hostile shelling in vicinity of batteries Interned to Shellfire.	
			Casualties: Gnr CALLUM. On draft of A/79 Sergt MULLEN E C/79 wounded Sergt CASEBROOK C/79 wounded CARTSIDE J. C/79 killed Carless A/13th HISCOCK P B/79 wounded W/2 A.C. WALKER B/79 appointed to Cadets	B/79

Lieut OC. C.H. RILEY 2nd in command

WAR DIARY
or
INTELLIGENCE SUMMARY.

(Erase heading not required.)

Army Form C. 2118.

Place	Date	Hour	Summary of Events and Information	Remarks and references to Appendices
Near LANGEMARCK	19		Enemy retired from our front batteries, into new line. 12 md night. Arranged for at intervals during day & night. Casualties: Gnr CRABB 9/79 (wounded) Gnr HIGGEN 9/79 (wounded R.13/79 (killed)	G/79
	20.	5.26 am	XIV Corps bombardment & emergency barrage began on XIV Corps front. 7/79 Bn came into action of new slots.	
			(15 km in front) Casualties: Gr DeVISS 6/79 (wounded) Gnr MURRAY R. (wounded) Gnr GREEN (wounded)	B/79
			Infantry carried out original plan 4.30 pm. S. 30 pm Gas shell by enemy midnight. Our f/79 Bn retired to centre site each fired 4 rounds of hurricane barrage at 3.30 pm.	
	21.	9.40 am 2 am 2.20 pm 3.30 pm	Top of 4.45 pm 9/79 heavy shelled with 7 in. Field	A/79
	22.	5.35 am 2nd Hour	The XIV Corps in conjunction with the XVIII Corps on right and the XXXVI Corps on left attacked. 2 divisions 34th on right — 35th on left. French Corps on left. Of the 79 Bn in the N.C. Brigades in the Right Group of & Artillery	
			Covering 35th Div. Carried out a creeping barrage advancing at the rate of 100 yards in 4 minutes. Creeping barrage 471 yards	C/79
			All 18 pdrs. Carried out on creeping barrage advancing at the rate of 100 yards in 4 minutes.	
			2 hours 18 min.	
			Infantry held up by Machine gun fire from line of concrete pill boxes place had not been captured & consolidated by Infantry although Div. reported this all objectives	
			Division say night (18th) reached to (16) Very satisfactory in subsequent counter attack. Bn of 35th failed to	
			Casualties 7/79 Gnr Irwin & Gnr Drewitt wounded Barrage Satisfactory. Gallop not recovered. Killed Capt EDEN C W 9/79	F/79 G/79

Major CWTRYRNE
Capt McTAVISH
Gnr HENRY PENMAN & MCQUEEN FINNIE HASTON DALGETY HOLMES PICKERING MC TO BRENNAN GILFILLAN GRIERSON CLAPTON DEANE PITFIELD

(fund)

Ernn WODSGEL & HENLEY (6/79) CRAGGIE BLACK BUTCHER & PARKER

Bn: BROOKS F G/79

WAR DIARY
or
INTELLIGENCE SUMMARY.

(Erase heading not required.)

Army Form C. 2118.

Place	Date	Hour	Summary of Events and Information	Remarks and references to Appendices
Near Langemarck	22.		Casualties. 19/79 Wounded. Sergt. CLARK J. Bomdr. MILLARD W. Gnr. TICKELL H. Gnr. THURGOOD E.T. Sergt. RANKIN G. Gnrs. DELL, KING, HADLEY and RYAN. D/79. Killed " " Wounded "	WD
	23.	3 AM	79th Bde. were ordered to position previous recommended on the LANGEMARCK — POELCAPPELLE Road about SCHREIBOOM. The Battery succeeded in getting into position without casualties, the only platform for guns to fire on actually unsupported being on previous shell holes strutted with logs filled in. Portion of the guns being in full view of enemy, so that all around supplies had to be taken to guns at night. U. a moderate amount of gas shell. Killed, Bdr MILLS B/79.	WD
	24.	5 AM	Remaining guns of Bty Hostile later to position. Parts of track hurriedly fixed unable to rescue our present shell the Hours out of the mud of its position. Personnel of Battalion withdrawn to W.L. Battalion silent.	WD
	25.	4 PM	Personnel recalled to guns. Registrate carried out inter covering fire from the 78th F/13 and 231 Heavy Bty. Push + Shrapnel fire from the 78th Bde.	WD

WAR DIARY

INTELLIGENCE SUMMARY

Army Form C. 2118.

Place	Date	Hour	Summary of Events and Information	Remarks and references to Appendices
POELCAPPELLE	26	5.40 AM.	ZERO HOUR. The XIV Corps attached ourselves by XVIII Corps on the Right and 1st French Army on the Left. 78th & 79th & 65th Bde. R.G.A. formed the Right Group. 9th Corps Artillery opened the advance fire the 149 Siege Bn. (58th Div.) 79th the forward the Creeping Barrage, 79th Bn. devoted to Standing Barrage. The operation on our front was (lit) of almost immediate by M.G. fire from concrete huts & pill boxes, behind TURENNE CROSSING — STROP-BOSIE — & up to flanking fire from DYSON FARM. The enemy's losses were enormous and showed them, for the Italian state of his mind, making to found almost always was has valiant impetuosity faith to find men at the same price as our Creeping Barrage. 79th Bn. Cease fire at 8.40 pm & renewed Schedule at 5pm. 79th Bn. return reported for defence of the line & turn of S.O.S. 79th Battalion fired.	MAP
	27		"	MAP
	28			MAP
	29			
	30	5.50 AM.	ZERO HOUR. 17th Division attacked by XVIII Corps on our right. 79th Bn. S.O.S. on his front. 17th Div. took over to 3am 29th. 79th Bn. returned to Rest.	MAP

Army Form C. 2118.

WAR DIARY
or
INTELLIGENCE SUMMARY.
(Erase heading not required.)

Instructions regarding War Diaries and Intelligence Summaries are contained in F. S. Regs., Part II and the Staff Manual respectively. Title pages will be prepared in manuscript.

Place	Date	Hour	Summary of Events and Information	Remarks and references to Appendices
POELCAPPELLE	31.		79th Bde silent. Ammunition taken up to gun positions now amounts to 900 RDS/gun.	
		4 pm	Personnel of D/79 withdrawn to rest with troops line.	
			A/79 4 guns in action	
			B/79 5 guns in action	
			C/79 2 guns —	
			All the remaining guns have previously been damaged or destroyed by shelling.	WP
		10.30 pm	Spasms of enemy GOTHA aeroplanes bombed the troops lines at ELVERDINGHE.	
			Casualties Killed 3 OR A/79. Horses killed 57.	
			honored 30 OR A/79. Horses wounded 32.	
			wounded 3 OR B/79.	

Nov. 1st 1917.

Lieut Col. R.F.A
Comdg 79th F.A.B

Army Form C. 2118.

WAR DIARY
or
INTELLIGENCE SUMMARY.
(Erase heading not required.)

79 PTB APPENDIX OCTOBER 1917

Place	Date	Hour		Remarks and references to Appendices

I. Ammunition expended October 1917
   A. 25920 AX 11670 BX 7900 CHEMICAL 1320

II. Casualties during OCTOBER
   Killed Officers. NIL O.R. 16
   Wounded Officers. 5 O.R. 129.

III. Strength from Return.
   Officers. 1 O.R. 24.

IV. Casualties to Horses & Mules
   Killed or Died 54
   Wounded 34
   Evacuated to M.V.S. 17.

Nov 1st 1917.

Signature
Russell Major
Comm'g 79 PTMB.

WAR DIARY
or
INTELLIGENCE SUMMARY

Army Form C. 2118.

Vol 28
10th Bde RHA

Place	Date	Hour	Summary of Events and Information	Remarks and references to Appendices
SCHREIBOOM, NEW POELCAPPELLE	1.		Batteries in action but silent. LANGEMARCK – POELCAPPELLE Rd. Battery Hqrs in EAGLE TRENCH. 12 guns in action by Hqrs. B/79, H/79 at ADELPH HOUSE. C.3.b.15.70. (Sheet 28 N.W.) D/79 resting at transport lines. Bdr FORSYTH L.D. (H/79) wounded. Cannalls Bdr JOY cut.	A/73
	2.		Batteries silent. Relief personnel Judgment/wounded. Gun cores & H/79) killed. Including gun NIGHT H/79 wounded.	H/79
	3.		" "	
	4.		" "	
	5.	6 am	20 enemy aircraft attacking army arm Rglt. to 79 N Bdn from enemy trenches to 45 min. shelling on SO.T. bns at 6am (Germ) guns white to slightly on an 'proche.' Battery silent.	H/79
	6.		D/79 wth H Hindges BEWL withd. further casualties	
	7.	1 am	Batteries left wartime pos. C/79 1 am to 2 am. B/79. 2. 15 am 4 am to 6 am A/79 4 am. Withdrawal almost without casualties. 5 men unknown.	H/79
	8.	9 am	Bde moved to PROVEN. Staying arm routes into hills 2 mls east of PROVEN for the night.	
	9.	9.15am	Bde moved to OCHTEZEELE. Reaches OCHTEZEELE at 3 pm.	
	10.		Bde resting reputting at OCHTEZEELE o/Major WATH GUISE MC reports from Base terminations A/79	A/79
	11.		o/M R.C. Worther adjuncts 2nd in cmd. Capt from CARVER went to Base.	

Army Form C. 2118.

INTELLIGENCE SUMMARY.

(Erase heading not required.)

Place	Date	Hour	Summary of Events and Information	Remarks and references to Appendices
OCHTEZEELE	12		Bn resting, refitting.	WD?
	13		Bde resting. Training commenced under Battln arrangements.	
	14		Bn refitting & training. 6 15pdr howitzers 1076 #4 = ABA	
	15		Bn refitting from 7 hours each to workshops ARMERIE to overhaul	
	16		Marching from training	
	17		Bn. Refitting & training. (96 Reinforcements received.)	WD?
	18		" "	
	19		" "	
	20		" "	
	21		" "	
	22		" "	
	23		(44 hours + 2 10pr howitzer to C/276 4 pdr)	WD?
	24			
	25			
	26			
	27			

Army Form C. 2118.

WAR DIARY
or
INTELLIGENCE SUMMARY.
(Erase heading not required.)

Place	Date	Hour	Summary of Events and Information	Remarks and references to Appendices
ECHTELZEELE	Nov 28		Brigade Resting + Training	
	29		— do —	
	30		— do —	

1st Decr. 1917

J M Welwood Lieut RTA
for Lieut Col Cmdg
79th I.B. R.T.A.

Army Form C. 2118.

WAR DIARY
or
INTELLIGENCE SUMMARY.

(Erase heading not required.)

79th T.M.B.   NOVEMBER 1917

Place	Date	Hour	Summary of Events and Information	Remarks and references to Appendices
			HUGEN DIX	
		I	Ammunition Expended November 1917.	
			18·34 A 171 AX 480 BX	
		II	Casualties :-	
			KILLED Officers Nil OR 1	
			WOUNDED Officers Nil OR 11	
			ACCIDENTALLY KILLED OR 1	
		III	Wastage from Sickness	
			Officers Nil OR 24	
		IV	Casualties to Horses Mules	
			Killed and Died 8	
			Wounded 3	
			Evacuated (MVS) 62	

J.M. Macleod Lieut
Lt Col. O.C. 79 TMB
1st Dec. 1917

WAR DIARY or **INTELLIGENCE SUMMARY.** 79th BDE. R.F.A.

DECEMBER 1917

Place	Date Dec.	Hour	Summary of Events and Information	Remarks and references to Appendices
OCHTEZEELE	1st		Brigade in out billets, refitting & training	WD
	2		"	
	3			
	4			
	5			
	6			
	7			
	8			
	9 " to 15 "		"	WD
	10		2nd Lt. V.C.L. Eastman left for England on 1 month course with V.C. Brind (Brigade Command) 2 MTB.	
	16"	9 A.M.	79th Div. Artillery marched out — 79th NOTRDAMEENIE — POCHTEZEELE — via THEROVANNE — via BABLINGHEM.	WD
CRECQUES			79th Bde. went into billets for 1 night at CRECQUES and REBECQUES	
	17th	8 A.M.	March continued through by PIPS to the VALHUON stopping area.	WD
			79th Bde. billets in SAINS-LES-PERNES and TANGRY. Snow fell all day.	
TANGRY	18"		Bde. rested.	
	19"		March resumed to the ETREE-WAMIN area via SI POL and FREVENT. Snow covered and frozen roads made the trek very difficult for the horses.	WD
	20"		79th Bde. billets in REBREUVIETTE.	WD
			Bde. resting.	

Army Form C. 2118.

WAR DIARY
or
INTELLIGENCE SUMMARY.
(Erase heading not required.)

Instructions regarding War Diaries and Intelligence Summaries are contained in F. S. Regs., Part II. and the Staff Manual respectively. Title pages will be prepared in manuscript.

Place	Date	Hour	Summary of Events and Information	Remarks and references to Appendices
REBREUVIETTE	21st		Brigade marched to FOSSEUX via REBREUVIETTE, MAYENVILLE & IVERGNY. Heavy rainfall. Units kept to main roads.	WD
FOSSEUX	22nd		Wet day. Snow.	
	23		Route Marching.	WD
	24th	10.30 am	Brigade marched to COURCELLES-LE-COMTE via BIENVILLERS	
	25th	11 am	Brigade marched to BOISLEUX COURT via BAPAUME	
	26th		Moved onward to headquarters at ETRICOURT	
HAVRINCOURT			Reconnaissance by Brigadier & 6th Div Artillery. (24th Bde.) near HAVRINCOURT. Gun Station for Btys. (Personnel and vehicles) attached for 18 Pr.	WD
forum line			1/ 24th Bde. A/73 when 118 Bde BS — (K.36.c.03.33)	
at BOISLEUX COURT			B/73 111.n.35 — (K.34.d.95.33)	
			C/79 112.BS — K.34.b.95.45	
			D/73 released 430 Hr 175 at K.34.b.95.45	
	27th		Guns exchanged. Gunner employed for night. Relief of 24th Bde completed by 1 am. 79th Bde. troops (part of 17th Infantry Group with A/ss & D/ss) Amm.Cols. b/ W. L. (W. C. Allcan) Bde. 1st Bde. & enemy to SS/BM (C.M. Bde.) & his 19th Div. Cav. Bde. Gen. Monkhouse. Harness tri guns to capture Shot in center select area. Delivery of guns reported. Commenced Front Artillery fire	WD
	28th			WD

WAR DIARY
or
INTELLIGENCE SUMMARY

Army Form C. 2118.

Place	Date	Hour	Summary of Events and Information	Remarks and references to Appendices
HAVRINCOURT	29.		Concentrated shots on other MG positions in HAVRINCOURT & CAINTAING and enemys Col/BtnHq.	W/2
	30.	6.30am	Enemy attacked 63rd Div on our Right. Battery opened a slow barrage in reply to SOS line. Thin ground mist. Casualties 2/Lt... wounded.	
			No 61206 Gnr Jew A (B/73) wounded.	
		7.15pm	Batteries supporting a creeping fire with 1/7 R.H. BLACK	
		9.30pm	OC A/73 advanced 1 gun an empty truck across and to near FLESQUIÈRES. This gun safely withdrawn to position. Range attack casualties began soon.	W/2
	31.		Major Gore N.C. (A/73) returns from ENGLAND. Resumes comm and Vice Burgess. Invalid (SICK) Extreme movement. 2/Lt IRVING 1/73 on to B/73 and joined a A(truck?) from into gun until... Gun withdrawn by gunners. 15 CAINTAING.	I/W2

W.A. Houghton
Capt R.F.A.
Officer
for Major Comdg 73 Bde

31/7/17

WAR DIARY
INTELLIGENCE SUMMARY

79th F.A.B.

APPENDIX — December 1917

I. Ammunition Expended December 1917

A 1250   AX 1633   BX 390

II. Casualties:
Killed   Officers NIL   O.R. NIL
          Officers NIL   O.R. 1
Wounded

III. Intake from Sickness:
Officers 1   O.R. 12.

IV. Casualties to horses and mules,
Strayed and died — 7
Evacuated to A.V.S. 22.
Killed or known drowned NIL.

M.A. Hangan
Capt & Adjt
for Major Cmdg, 79 FAB

1st Jan 1917

WAR DIARY or **INTELLIGENCE SUMMARY**

79 Bde RFA
Vol 30

Place	Date	Hour	Summary of Events and Information	Remarks and references to Appendices
HAVRINCOURT	1		Batteries in action between HAVRINCOURT and RIBECOURT. A/79 K.36.c 03.33 B/79 K.34 d 95.55 C/79 K.34 b 95.23 D/79 K.34 b 3545. (1 How near FLESQUIERES) Hqrs was at HINDENBURG LINE just immediately in front of A/79 position.	6/VII
			Wagon lines still at ETRICOURT	
	2.	3 pm	One Section junr B/79 relieved by junr 88th Bn RFA 19th Div. Artillery; 79th Bn Wagon lines moved to RUYAULCOURT	6/22
	3	3 pm	Remaining Section of 79th Bde relieved to ammunition section of RFA Bn. Personnel, ads, vehicles, guns, stores, wee exchanged.	
		4 pm	Relief complete. Batteries of the 79th Bde relieve one section per Bty of One Section per Bty of 41st Bn RFA, 2nd Div Arty in position about HERMIES.	
			Hqrs A/79 took over from 9th B5 K.25.c. 6040	
			B/79 " " " 16th735 K.25.c. 4050	6/III
			C/79 " " " 17/85 K.25.c. 0050	
			D/79 " " " 47th (How) B5 K.31.B 4060.	
			K 20 d 50 40 (1 How)	
			Hqrs at K.25 B 9070. Personal adj vehicles, guns, exchange supper.	
HERMIES	4.	1 pm	Relief of 41st Bn RFA complete. The 78 & 79 Bn take over 15-7 D.A Group (commanded by Lt Col K. & G. KIRBY) covering K.57th Bn of 17 Div. Brig. Gen. P. Walter Dso.	6/III

WAR DIARY or INTELLIGENCE SUMMARY

Army Form C. 2118.

Place	Date	Hour	Summary of Events and Information	Remarks and references to Appendices
HERMIES	5.		A little registration carried out; visibility very poor. Night harassing fire on approaches.	6022
	6.		Do. Do.	6022
	7.	3.25pm	3 Group Salvos on S.O.S. line of Infantry request for retaliation.	6022
		3.40pm	On K.10.a & K.16.B. (enemy suppers)	
		7pm	Harassing fire during night.	
	8.	9 am	17th Divl. Front inspected by 52nd Hy Bde. Arrgill. Escorted by 7th FAB and 57th Hy. Bde. a Representative of 79th SB. Major W.H. Gore M.C. and 29th Bde. Liaison Officer with 57th Bde.	6022
	9.	6 am	Bursts of 30 Pds Shrapnel per B5 infantry enemy trench in K.3.C. +two hundred of 20 Pds Bursts on trench junction in K.3.a.	6027
		9.45am	S.O.S. Barrage tested.	
		10.11.30am	Harassing fires on Cambrai Rd. fired a rehearsed during the morning. Exposes for front 16pdr in trenches in K.3.C.	
	15&7/h	Aright firing.	
			Commonwealth troops movement throughout the day; visibility very poor. Enemy attacked expected at dusk.	
	16.	8.30 pm	Heavy barrage for 10 min. by all Batteries on own & then enemy front line.	6022

Army Form C. 2118.

WAR DIARY
or
INTELLIGENCE SUMMARY.
(Erase heading not required.)

Instructions regarding War Diaries and Intelligence Summaries are contained in F. S. Regs., Part II. and the Staff Manual respectively. Title pages will be prepared in manuscript.

Place	Date	Hour	Summary of Events and Information	Remarks and references to Appendices
HERMIES.	11		Harassing fire carried on through the night 10/11th from own Arms.	
		5.30 am	Shot 3 rds from his own dug-outs in retaliation.	
		6.17 am	10 minutes bombardment and whole of the Corps front and shell trained for 300 yds.	WO2
		18 pm.	agusta S.O.S. line. No retaliation from enemy.	
	12		Lgth vary gd: all batteries obtained good accurate registration. 13/79 started to withdraw to run position of East side of the Canal about K.31.c. Called men a section each day. This broken as shots took in view to 13/79 ensuring its withdrawal of the other batteries in case of emergency. Night quiet.	WO2
	13		Destructive shot of SCOTT put. by C/75 ensuring also registration. Several parties of the enemy observed during the morning, found visible machine gun emplacements + super front in reply to C/75 WAFE. Harassing fire at night on enemy approaches.	WO2
	14		Harassing fire carried out by night and much as noun that by 1st enemy arty. activity expenditure approx 250 rds.	
	15		18 pr per Brs and 100 rds per How 13/5. 13/75 withdrawn to -	WO
	16		New christian Schul except for S.O.S. calls, returning to rest leave in England. Withdrawn front. Lt Colonel E. W. Homer, returning home through 10th Corps. M.C. Commanding.	

A 5834 Wt. W4973/M687 750,000 8/16 D.D. & L. Ltd. Forms/C.2118/13.

WAR DIARY or INTELLIGENCE SUMMARY

Army Form C. 2118.

Place	Date	Hour	Summary of Events and Information	Remarks and references to Appendices
HEBUTERNE	17		Harassing fire by night.	
	18		Defensive fire as per 18th Bde.	
	19		52nd Bde relief by 6th Bde. 51st Bde's secret station taken over by 52nd Bde at 5.50am 19th Bde serving 79th Bde & remained Battery HQrs moved Q.18.b by 10.5am. 79th Bn Battle HQ to be known: Mesnelette''	
	20		19th 79th Bde established near the Left Bys Bde HQ in Rt Canal Banks at J.36.b.2.3. mil	
	21			
	22nd to 31st		Average expenditure of 350 Rds 18Pr to 75Bn and 130 Rds Howitzer rounds. The amount expended in harassing fire by night on enemy's run defences & on his approaches back of C.T.S. (75%) and 25% remainder on Enemy, on a usual expectation to destroy particularly the enemy stores at about 6000 yds range. A/79 & B/79 4th Calibration fire 3rd carrying on. (Remedies funds rec'd from spares 073). Result satisfactory. Month closed with clear weather to register. Two O.P.'s manned always in daylight by OP. manning staff in strong teams and Batteries engaged chiefly in strong teams and registration.	

M.H. Thompson
Capt. RAJT.
C Linecill R.A. comd'g 79 FAB.

Army Form C. 2118.

WAR DIARY
or
INTELLIGENCE SUMMARY.
(Erase heading not required.)

79^ FA/B   APP #N/D   JANUARY 1918

I	Ammunition expended - January 1918
	A 4206 Ax 4720 Bx 2344 GAS 48.
II	Casualties. NIL
III	Wastage from Sickness. Officers: NIL
	O.R. : 23.
IV	Casualties Horses:
	Killed and wounded NIL
	Evacuated to M.V.S. 26
	Destroyed 3.

1st Feb. 1918.

W.H. Thompson.
CAPTAIN
T/Lt Col R.F.A.
Cmd'g 79 FA/B

Army Form C. 2118.

WAR DIARY
or
INTELLIGENCE SUMMARY.

(Erase heading not required.)

79ᵗʰ T.M.B.   FEBRUARY.

Place	Date	Hour	Summary of Events and Information	Remarks and references to Appendices
HERMIES	1		Batteries in action in following emplacements	
			A/79 K 25 c 5560 with forward section at K 25 a 3520	
			B/79 Q.I.A. 5075 (HIGH WOODS)	(W.D)
			C/79 K 25 c 0050	
			D/79 K 31 B 4060. with 1 forward How. at K.25 d 5045	
			Aeroplane on Counter Bank at J.36.b.3.2. Wagon lines at VÉLU WOOD	
			Harassing fire carried out on enemy thoroughfares known to be working	
			on T.M. Emps. Suspects enemy relief in GRAINCOURT SECTOR,	
			Harassing shots fired 6.657 him	
			Lt A.W. Gordon 79 T.M.B. left forward a dying from wds. rec'd himself	
			in the HERMIES-GRAINCOURT Road to the ambulance at	
			50ᵗʰ Inf Bn. Relieved K.52 by Bn. & covered by 79ᵗʰ Bn.	
	2		Normal harassing fire by day & night.	MMS
	3		In addition to the usual harassing fire, A/79 engaged twin TM	
			emplacement on Spoil Bank at K3C 8.4. These were considerably	
			damaged. 7 direct hits being obtained.	
	4		Normal hostility going for TM emplacement & fired at 10.30 am on account of	MMS
			heavy hostile TM bombardment at dawn. Enemy working party caught	
			in it, several casualties observed also direct hit on an active TM	
		am		
	5	12.45	Enemy TMs very active. Known TMs engaged.	MMS
		1.45		
		6.6.45	Heavy TM bombardment along Divisional Front, extending F Bn on our	MMS

Army Form C. 2118.

WAR DIARY
or
INTELLIGENCE SUMMARY.
(Erase heading not required.)

Instructions regarding War Diaries and Intelligence Summaries are contained in F. S. Regs., Part II. and the Staff Manual respectively. Title pages will be prepared in manuscript.

Place	Date 1918	Hour	Summary of Events and Information	Remarks and references to Appendices
HERMIES	26.5		Left Batteries maintained protective barrage on SOS Line during night bombardment. Usual day/night fire.	MM
	6	6.30pm	B/179 took out Sniping gun with 100 Rds on Cross Roads E.29.a.5?	MM
	7		Normal harassing fire. Visibility low.	
	8	2 am	Sniping gun taken out by A/179 & K/9 a. fired 100 Rds on Tranch E.29.a.5.9 – E.29.A.3.5	MM
			Usual harassing fire	
		11pm	Sniping Gun (M/179) 100 Rds Cross Rds ; factory E.29.a.	MM
	9		Normal harassing fire by day by night. Batteries carried out practise shoots being raided lby	MM
	10			
	11			
	12	5.60a	Enemy reported to be in no mans land cutting our wire. Protective Barrage opened for 20 minutes – 78th Bde ½ 73rd Bde Slow to – no attack developed. It was later found that the enemy (who were taken prisoner) had lost themselves & become caught in our wire.	MM
	13	10am	Command of CANAL SECTOR passed from 57th Inty Bde to 51st Inty Bde.	MM
	13		Usual harassing fire carried out. Visibility good.	
	14			
	15		Looking parties engaged.	

Army Form C. 2118.

WAR DIARY
or
INTELLIGENCE SUMMARY.
(Erase heading not required.)

Instructions regarding War Diaries and Intelligence Summaries are contained in F.S. Regs., Part II. and the Staff Manual respectively. Title pages will be prepared in manuscript.

Place	Date 1918	Hour	Summary of Events and Information	Remarks and references to Appendices
HERMIES	Aug 16	2–5 pm	D/79 carried out a distributive shoot against Snipers post and rifle battery on Hermies buttresses of distant canal bridge & K.9.b. 200 rounds were fired. 17 direct hits causing considerable damage were observed. Front line was cleared for this shoot.	JM
			Enemy paid considerable attention to the batteries round SOURBS COPSE during the day, using chiefly 4.2's & a few 5.9's. No damage caused. At 11 pm a short burst of gas shell near D/79. Gothas very active during the evening. Casualties	MM
	17	7 p.m.	Concentrated bursts of fire (act DA Theories) on account of Enemy rally in this trak. Casualties 3572 Gr. W.S POPE strh 27537 for SPROOM at ground store.	JM
	17			ms
	19			JM
	19		Normal Harassing fire by day & night. Gothas active on evenings of 17 & 18.	
	20			
	21		Enemy fire by day slacker. 18/19th Battery in turn took turns to extra attn to 2nd link to keep enemy communications.	
	22			
	23		Shoots T. M. Cams Cutralls during day to our front	
	24		and Garrison. Registration by 7 p/79 then and	—
	25		Heavy Artillery	WD
	26			
	27			
	28			

W.A. Thompson
Lt Col
R.A. 79th FAB

Army Form C. 2118.

WAR DIARY
or
INTELLIGENCE SUMMARY.

(Erase heading not required.)

79th FAB   APPENDIX — FEBRUARY 1918

Place	Date	Hour	Summary of Events and Information	Remarks and references to Appendices

I. Ammunition expended — January 1918

A. 3590   AX 3254   BX 2519.   Chemical 150

II. Casualties   Killed NIL
   Wounded 2 OR

III. Wastage from Sickness   9 OR

IV. Casualties to Horses.
   Killed or wounded NIL
   Died 1
   Lost 1
   Evacuated to M.V.S. 23

W.H. Thompson
Capt. & Adjt.
79th FAB

2nd Feb 1918
for Lt. Col. Cmdg. 79th FAB.

17th Div.

Headquarters,

79th BRIGADE, R.F.A.

M A R C H

1 9 1 8

WAR DIARY
INTELLIGENCE SUMMARY

79th Bde R.F.A.   March   17 Dec

Place	Date	Hour	Summary of Events and Information	Remarks and references to Appendices
HERMIES	1.		Batteries in action in same positions as in February. Approx lines VELU WOOD i.e. Ref. map. 57c N.E.	
	2.		HdQrs. J. 36. b. 2020.	
	3.		A/79 K. 25. c. 5080. forward section K 25 d 3020.	
	4.		B/79 Q. 1. a. 5095. (2 HIGH WOODS) "Silent portion"	
	5.		C/79 K. 25. c. 0050.	
	6.		D/79 K. 31. b. 4660. (1 Hdqr formed at K 20 d 5040)	WD
	7.		Defensive scheme consisting mostly of S.O.S. lines and intermittent small fire	
	8.		harassing shoots by F.O.O's and unintelligent hate T.M.S.	
	9.		Night firing - about 250 Rs per night fires on known enemy	
	10.		communication approaches and supply tracks and	
	11.		materialize T.M.S.	
			Clear weather was maintained with the infantry successful experiments	
			with infantry O.P's in engaging fleeting targets.	
			Also, 1 infantry officer was attached to each "active" battery of	to 42.
			the Bde for instruction: - relief once a week.	
			Much work was done during the period to strengthen battery	
			positions by means of dug-outs and wire in front of the guns	
			and on its flanks, whilst the materials approaches & positions	
			has carried on with all possible speed.	
			500 R.D fired from gunners list 15th march opened	
			in preparation for enemy possible defensive offensive.	
			HERMIES - BERTINCOURT line

Army Form C. 2118.

WAR DIARY
or
INTELLIGENCE SUMMARY.

79th FAB   Month: March

Place	Date	Hour	Summary of Events and Information	Remarks and references to Appendices
HERMIES	12.		Special orders issued to all units of the Corps in anticipation of an attack on the morning of the 13th. (From information received, from prisoners). Harrassing fire from dusk thru last night (modified by S.O.S and Counter Preparation) bombardments by the artillery of V Corps. Artillery carried out from 1.30 a.m. to 6.30 a.m. 13th. A night June Harrassment.	
	13.		(On the night of the 12th/13th March CPS posts patrolled and to arms between the minutes of the cover was launched to the fire of: L/M Pickets & phosgene canister & smoke bombs & secondary bombardment by Cairelli. Casualties 418483 Cpl. OAKES C.R. 98347 Gnr BROWN S. 142617 Dr. GREEN F. 198933 Gnr PICK H.W.	WD
			Day fairly quiet. After light fighting enemy attempts to our right and T.M. supplements bombardment to B/79.	MWD
	14.		Capt bombardment. Enemy given counter thro phrs its night 13/14 Fire stopped at 6.45 a.m. till Rest of Day very quiet. Weather very foggy.	WD

WAR DIARY
or
INTELLIGENCE SUMMARY.

(Erase heading not required.)

Army Form C. 2118.

Place	Date	Hour	Summary of Events and Information	Remarks and references to Appendices
HERMIES.	15		Intense harassing fire carried out by night in many different	
	16		places all through. Some hours of day light very carefully observed	
	17		although front and outmanned arcs of view engaged by batteries.	(WD?)
	18		Work of consolidating conne positions still carried on.	
	19		Attack expected morning of 20th a 21st March. (from previous statements)	
	20			
	21	4.30 am	Enemy attacks on 3rd and 5th Army fronts. On 17th Div front bombardment by Yprite, Phosgene and other heavy shelling	
			with some times a sheen fire in considerable volume on the Canal Sector, and on part of Communication. (Shell batteries escaped with Cangor Sector and on 50th Div Bde in the Lys-Canal Sector RPs covered by 3rd Bde, elevation 79th RPs covered " " " Left Canal Sector.	
			78th " " " 82nd "	
			Batteries maintained harassing finish fire from 5am on SOS lines occasionally quickening up to SOS rates of fire; until about 11 noon	(WD)
			Down through mm. Three 7 mm loads up in Lys line and ws. OT; also a General bombardment of the enemy mm. A further attack.	
			In effective heavy and Contain'g fire bombardment all day to keep down the fire of our field slow from the line ; with searchlight	
	9.0 pm		while a small outpost front between both batteries to support our RA" reserve Buzon nearl'g from CRA for batteries HERM (156 - TRESCAULT line directly before and bestring for before illuminate to confirm with 5th Div in my Lyr	Caines, etc R43 H/ RH BL M12
				I. OTR
			9.30 am our to slow and incorrect passing the from the N.E.	15 th

WAR DIARY or INTELLIGENCE SUMMARY

Army Form C. 2118.

Place	Date	Hour	Summary of Events and Information	Remarks and references to Appendices
HERMIES	22		Platoons retaken in turn 1st Reserve positions. Approx. 3 x 0's & 45 went to HERMIES and away the Canal Slag Heap; 3/74 unable to extricate for Infantry HQ. remained with 50th Inf. Bn. HQ now Canal Group, all grey up. Orders to the N. westward of the 59th Div. an now left 17th Div. left. Further concentration in HERMIES minus by the permanent garrison N. 51st Res. (7th trenches & 18th Shannons Frontier).	
			79th Rse covers HERMIES. Operation from S. successive attacks on HERMIES were broken the own Lewis & Artillery & MG fire.	6200
			The MGPt Lithium, where it seemed fairly proven moving halted HERMIES from the north right.	
	22	10.1pm	Inspection withdrawn to a Ruyaulcourt – VILLERS-AU-FLOS. Orders seems for troops to withdraw into S.P. BARTA & Mt. GARFORTH. Shel kept owner to further withdrawal of our troops.	
			HQ AIRCRAFT evacuated.	
	23.	4am	Oden received from CRA the Retained to withdraw to defend the GREEN LINE positions. 17th Div. not. Move through the 2nd Division defending the GREEN LINE, army to further retirement of the Division & outlying Batteries R 79 Bn returned in echelon. D/75 and B/75 return hast covered by A & C/75. O/75, then retained with A.D. x Sept-B/74.	WD2
			An further march in echelon past S.P. VELU WOOD with this flank extending to R.G. Detachment 17 5/75 but extends Trey R. d 5/75. Connected to suspect knowing commissioner at the enemy attacking left wing this body on. Four Bytl. coly from Bytl. S. army onto	

WAR DIARY or INTELLIGENCE SUMMARY

Army Form C. 2118.

Place	Date	Hour	Summary of Events and Information	Remarks and references to Appendices
VILLERS - AU - FLOS	23.	3pm	B/79 returns to remainder of the Brigade in position N. of Villers. Battery took up action immediately S. of Villers-au-Flos under heavy shell fire.	
		4pm	A & D/79 with the return marched to 2nd Divl Arty. Were given instructions alongside on the 79th Army F.A. Bde Group.	
		6pm	B & C/79 (Lt. Col. K.G. Pemple). All batteries were covering operation of the Green Line held by 2nd Division. Bunch of H.E. throughout the night. Burst in SOS line.	WD
		8pm	All batteries came again into the Command of CRA 17th Div & switching their guns to the South covers the advance of the 57" Bde (17" Div) to LES SAILLY-SAILLISEL and opposite tried with Gth Divn on our right.	
	24.		Officers patrols sent forward to clear up the situation & barrage established. Seems the party of the enemy expects advance of the enemy.	WD
			The Right flank of the 57th Bde has by necessity to withdraw followed by general withdrawal to 17 & Divs. Batteries return to positions near LE TRANSLOY West of the BAPAUME Rd. To cover the retirement of 57th Bde through from ROCAVINY to the BAPAUME Rd.	
		11am		
		4pm	The field Batteries retire further via B.EAULEY COURT to positions near LGNY-TILLOY from which they could support SLOPES on LE TRANSLOY	

Army Form C. 2118.

WAR DIARY
or
INTELLIGENCE SUMMARY.
(Erase heading not required.)

Instructions regarding War Diaries and Intelligence Summaries are contained in F.S. Regs., Part II. and the Staff Manual respectively. Title pages will be prepared in manuscript.

Place	Date	Hour	Summary of Events and Information	Remarks and references to Appendices
LIGNY-TILLOY	24	6-7 am	B/79 & B/72 fired rounds all the ammn from the position into PUCQUINY before retiring whilst B/71 & their batteries to retire from nearly 300 Rd per open sights at the enemy debouching from LE TRANSLOY withdrew on to BAPAUME road towards BEAUCOURT. All Batteries then retired via LE SARS to COURCELLETTE to cover 17th Divl infantry retiring on MARTINPUICH	A.172
		10 pm	17th Batteries took up position of readiness on the BAPAUME-ALBERT road near COURCELLETTE.	
POZIERES	25	1 Am	Batteries took up positions at POZIERES to cover "ANSON" Bttn R.N. Division (63rd) helding a line in ridge south of MARTINPUICH and supports of 51st & 9th Bde.	
		6 Am	Guns switched further south to cover to ST. PIERRE the advance into line on right of 63rd Naval Division and LLOYD ridge south of CONTALMAISON	
		11 Am	Guns of the division on our left (47 ?) withdrawing & were considered advisable to more batty positions further S.W. along the ALBERT Road on an left flank was exposed.	A.172
LA BOISSELLE		The Bde continued retire by batteries to positions S.W. of POZIERES covering our own infantry & the continuance to the Rev Found transport to day out the high ground in front of CONTALMAISON. Then remaining there till 6 pm when troops given for retirement for remnad to enemy attack in the afternoon.	

D.D.A.L. London, E.C.
(A7004) Wt W1772/M9091 750m/co 5/17 Sch 52 Forms/C2118/14

WAR DIARY
or
INTELLIGENCE SUMMARY.
(Erase heading not required.)

Army Form C. 2118.

Place	Date	Hour	Summary of Events and Information	Remarks and references to Appendices
ALBERT	25	7 pm	The Brigade took up positions astride the BAPAUME-ALBERT Road just due East of ALBERT to cover the 12th Division. (17th Division withdrew from the line West of ALBERT) Orders received to withdraw batteries to Forceville astride the ALBERT—	
	26.	3 am	BAPAUME Road just West of ALBERT. 7 Bm — covered to 35th Bde of 12th Division. Orders to G.O.C. 35th Bde were also to his Column of the ANCRE trying to conform, they were so weak that the batteries were told close with them effectively in order from rest of ALBERT. 38e zone ALBERT to AVELUT inclusive. Batteries withdrew to positions East of SENLIS.	
BOUZINCOURT	27.	10 am	BOUZINCOURT. 5 guns in an E of the craters to shut off your sights. Situation from hill shop away on enemy approach to the main Enemy succeeded in crossing the river during the night N of ALBERT. From North of the 12th Division which but pressed to of ALBERT. 17th Dir: 10th Bm from 12 Div.) 7/ Bm covered 50th Bm (Left Bde). Night quiet.	
	28		Xlium barrage fire kept up all day; & many enemy parties were on Hipwood 7 pm Gen advance to withdraw to forekan or SENLIS was ordered & batteries at midnight of 1 hour.	

Date	Hour	
29.	1 Am.	All batteries in action at SENLIS, covering 50th Inf Bde.
		HQ. at V.16.b.7.2
		A/75 at V.16.d.3.3
		B/75 at V.17.c.1.55
		C/75 at V.17.c.4.4
		D/75 at V.16.d.9.8

Reported enemy advance. Harassing fire throughout the night.

30. At 4 am. pts on left flank (E. Yorks) captured. Batteries kept in action on Houeson pin in a enemy apparent to their pts. preparations for our counter attack on the 31st.

31. 5.30 am. to Yorks. attacked to regain positions of left front. by 75 & 77 Bns RFA & MG. to "YACK-YPR" trench & supports
Attack failure owing to (1) M.G. fire on our left flank
(2) Smoke and later enemy interdiction
(3) Heavy loss amongst attacking troops before start.

W.A. Thompson
Capt. & Adj.
75th Bde R.F.A.

20 April 1918.

79th Bde R.F.A. - Warthois - March

Appendix.

I. Ammunition expended March 1918 (all recent entries)
   A. 6000 (approx) A.X. 6000 (approx) B.X. 3000 (approx)

II. Casualties.
    Killed   Officers 1   O.R. 1
    Wounded   Officers 2   O.R. 28 (including 9 gunners)

III. Wastage from Sickness.
     Officers 1   O.R. 26.

IV. Horse Casualties.
    Killed   20
    Wounded   1.
    Evacuated 11. (to M.V.S.)

W.A. Thompson
Capt & Adjt/-
79th Bde R.F.A.

2.4.18

Index

SUBJECT.

No.	Contents.	Date.
	A few notes by Major C.H.A. Huxtable on Operations of 79th Brigade R.F.A. (17th Division) V Corps, 21st - 23rd March 1918.	

[*Not for Visitors*]

A few notes by Major C.H.A.Huxtable DSO.MC.
on the operations of the 79th Brigade R.F.A.
(17th Division) V.Corps front, 21st-23rd
March 1918.

The writer of these few notes commanded during these operations B.Battery, 79th Brigade.

Owing to the batteries of the Brigade being much separated during these operations, I am only able to give in detail facts concerning the movements and actions of the battery over which I had command.

21st March 1918.

At the commencement of the German offensive on the morning of the 21st March the batteries of the 17th Divisional Artillery were dotted about in positions on either side of the Canal du Nord, with Hermies as our northern boundary and the High Woods of Havrincourt Wood as the southern.

During the 21st all batteries were fairly heavily shelled, but without much material damage. All batteries maintained their fire on barrage lines practically throughout the whole day.

By the evening the enemy's fire became less and we were all very pleased with the result of the day's fighting on our actual front, not knowing, of course, what had happened to the north and south of our corps.

We were all much surprised when orders were received about 10 p.m. to retire to our next positions on the northern back of the valley running eastwards from Velu Wood to the Canal du Nord.

The retirement was carried out by all batteries during the night without loss.

22nd March 1918.

This was a quiet day, a steady barrage was maintained

Notes by Major C.H.A. Huxtable
on Ops of 79 Bde RFA (17 Divn)
21-23 Mch 1918

Alteration on p 2, line 9
from bottom. Alter to
read.
"....... on a line almost due
EAST....."

 not WEST.

all day in front of the 7/Lincoln and 6/Dorset who were defending Hermies.

We were also able to co-operate effectively with the infantry in repelling several small attacks made by the enemy during the day.

23rd March 1918.

The morning broke clear and we were all well satisfied with the results of the previous day's work.

However, about 9 a.m. all batteries, except mine, received orders to retire and rendezvous at Rocquigny, or thereabouts, as quickly as possible. My orders were that my battery should cover the retirement of the 51st Brigade of infantry from Hermies, which would take place at 1 p.m. After that hour I was given to understand that I should try and get back as best I could.

During the morning a protective barrage was maintained by my battery in front of the infantry. About noon groups of Argyll & Sutherland Highlanders were passing through my battery, and away on the left at Velu and Lebucquière heavy fighting appeared to be going on.

The Highlanders informed me that there were no troops left behind them, and I found this to be true on sending out a patrol from the battery. I was therefore faced with the position of having to maintain a barrage on a line almost due EAST, while the enemy were approaching me unopposed from the north.

I therefore decided to retire by sections to the other side of the valley, from which position I could just as easily maintain my barrage in front of Hermies, and at the same time the enemy would have to traverse the open valley before being able to attack me, instead of being able to approach me unseen as they could in my other position.

This change of position was made by me about 12.30 p.m. and the guns and wagons followed a route quite close to the eastern edge of the Velu Wood. The teams were not fired at and personally I do not think that there were any Germans in the wood till well after 1 p.m.

This does not agree with the Official History p.13.

My new position was some 500 yards due east of the southern end of Velu Wood, and in front of the Green Line.

From this position a protective barrage was fired until about 1.30 p.m. when large forces of the enemy were seen approaching in lines from the north.

These troops were engaged by me over open sights; my opening range was 1,500 yards and gun fire was resorted to. However these troops continued to advance, although considerable casualties were inflicted on them until my range had been reduced to 500 yards, when the enemy broke and scattered, part going into the wood while others sheltered in a sunken road in the Grand Ravie N.

It probably was the latter party that inflicted the losses on the 10/Sherwood Foresters (see p.13 of history). The hour was now about 2 p.m. and I began to think that it was time that I should endeavour to extricate my battery from the dangerous position it was in, as by that time the infantry must have retired from Hermies.

I therefore ordered up my gun and firing battery wagon teams by sections. I got four guns away with their ammunition wagons without loss, but, when the last section teams came up, heavy machine-gun fire was opened on us from Velu Wood.

The wagon teams of both guns got away safely but the horses of both gun teams were hit. The centres of the fifth gun team were brought down, but this team was quickly made into a four-horse team and got away safely. The sixth gun, however, gave more trouble, and in the end was hauled away by the two wheelers and with the gunners man-handling the wheels.

We then passed through the Green Line, which at that spot in front of Bertincourt was then well-manned by our troops, a battalion of Gloucestershires, which I understood belonged to the 19th Division.

My battery, having carried out its orders, then proceeded to join up with the rest of the brigade at Rocquigny.

I had expended all my ammunition in repelling the attack at Velu Wood, and therefore on my way back I sent my empty wagons to the dump at Ytres where we filled up. The dump was found absolutely deserted.

On p.18 of the History I see it is stated that the dumps at Ytres were empty. There were enough shells for my battery anyhow at 3 p.m. or later that day.

While my men were filling the wagons at the dump the properties of one of the Divisional Concert Parties were found, and all the drivers at once proceeded to dress up in the various fancy dresses and funny hats. Their appearance on return to the guns was particularly grotesque. I tell this story to show how good was the morale of the troops.

Later in the day I found the brigade staff and was ordered to go to Villers au Flos in order to strengthen the 77th A.F.A.Brigade.

Close to the village my battery went into action. Very little firing was done during the night as no one

seemed to know where our troops were. The night passed
quietly, and on the morning of the 24th March my battery
rejoined the 79th Brigade at Le Transloy.

(sgd) C.H.A.Buxtable.
Late Officer Commanding B/79
R.F.A.B.

17th Divisional Artillery

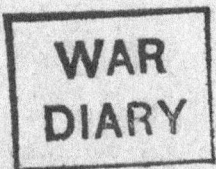

79th BRIGADE R. F. A.

APRIL :1 9 1 8

Appendix :- see last page

APRIL 1918.   79th F.A.B.

Place	Date		Events.
SENLIS	1st	Jour:	

79th Bde. in action at SENLIS supporting the 8th inf. Bde. The villages of the villages of SENLIS & WARLOY and VARENNES. Harassing fire carried out by enemy approaches to hu positions from the main from counter-btys. ALBERT. 36th Bde. (21st Division) to left Bde. in the line covering 79th Bde. Majr. CARR takes liason between units with 79th Bde. HQ. at SENLIS CHATEAU. Harrassing fire kept up on night in anticipation of further enemy attack an an endeavor on the high ground east of BOUZINCOURT. [WAR]

2.
3.
4. 10 pm 79 Bde HQ moved across the village & inspects to the trench near the Batteries.
    6 am Intense bombardment by enemy commences on the division on our right and left.
5. 7 am Heavy barrage in an form transfered line; transferon broken near the pt in Hy GOSIE M.C. & 2/Lieut J.B. JONES was brought the predicaments at A/79 junction. The major pickets & dispatch an orderly to gun transferon. 9.15 am Enemy transferon over support finds hundred. So I signal received to all Bde. batteries was to go in firing to cover the infantry by the Bde. suffered heavy casualties. Majr V.C. BRUCE C and 7 D/79 wounded, also 2/Lieuts H.C. IRVING. A.R. URQUHART. G.M.R. BEARD. wounded and 22 other ranks killed. 3 sergeants, 2 corporals & 2 gun-dealers. Batteries continued to support the infantry throughout the morning. [WAR]

WAR DIARY
INTELLIGENCE SUMMARY.
(Erase heading not required.)

Army Form C. 2118.

17R

Place	Date 1918	Hour	Summary of Events and Information	Remarks and references to Appendices
SENLIS	Sept 5	1 pm.	5. Headquarters moved to WARLY - SENLIS Road VISC S.9. Communications being almost impossible from previous HQ. 8/19 moved to broken outskirts of SENLIS. Hostile shelling slackened but did not cease till night fall.	WD1
	6.		Night of 5/6 was quiet - usual harassing fire carried out. Visibility (?) during the day. No movement could be observed.	
	7.	5 am	5.30am Barrage on SOS lines and to 300 yards behind, H.A. cooperating. No fire counter preparation from 5.10 - 6.25 am. The day was quiet. Some shelling of SENLIS.	WD2
	8.		On the night 7/9th. 37" Infantry Brigade relieved 36". Intermittent shelling on forward areas during the day.	
	9.	12.15pm - 3pm	Gas bombardment of SENLIS and valley running SE from it. Three calibres used - 4.2" 5.9" and 8". The latter containing a new gas, similar to mustard but gas in odour, but having painful effect on the eyes for 72 hours. No serious results. In small concentrations there were about 20 many mustard gas shell and air shrapnel. One 8" direct hit (gas shell) on 8/19 HQ caused casualties - Lt. B.M. HALLIWARD killed, Major CHIMHUXTABLE wounded. Capt J. SMITH RAMC wounded and 3 OR wounded. These were all buried by the shell. Casualties to OR today 37, mostly gas, a large proportion being men of 8/19 who had to work without masks to dig their officers out. Night firing increased + 250 rounds per Battery.	WD3
	10.	4.30 am	4. Above fired gas into 2m. and north of ALBERT. The day was quiet. During expected enemy attack on a large scale, night firing 10/11, increased to 300 rounds per Battery. Shelling of SENLIS starts area(?) quiet, visibility good.	

Army Form C. 2118.

WAR DIARY
or
INTELLIGENCE SUMMARY.
(Erase heading not required.)

Place	Date 1917	Hour	Summary of Events and Information	Remarks and references to Appendices
SENLIS	Apl 12		Night firing again 300 rounds per Battery owing to expected enemy attack. The day was quiet. Visibility very good + considerable aerial activity.	MW
		9.30pm	77th Bde relieved by 34th Army F.A. Bde. Guns were not exchanged. 77th Bde withdrew to wagon lines, Hqrs at WARLOY. Bde in Corps Mobile Reserve	
TOUTENCOURT AREA	Apl 13.		Brigade resting and refitting at wagon lines. A/79 near VARENNES, B/79 in WARLOY C/79 + D/79 near VARENNES, B/79	MW
	14		Brigade resting and refitting A/79 moved to HARPONVILLE, HQrs + TOUTENCOURT B/79 to LE QUESNOYE (TOUTENCOURT - PUCHEVILLERS ROAD)	
	15			Lt Col K Hopwood passed
	16			Major CARVER 2/Lts
	17		Brigade Resting and Refitting.	HOY, HOPSON + CARNE
	18			K Hospital passed
	19			
	20			MW
	21			
	22		Brigade & Battery Commanders reconnoitred positions of 77th A.F.A. Bde.	
	23	3pm	One Section per battery relieved corresponding section of 77th A.F.A. Bde.	MW
ENGLEBELMER	24	9pm	Relief completed, and responsibility for defence of line assumed by 79th Bde, who became left forward Brigade covering left Infantry Bde. (156 J.B.) of 35th Division. Headquarters at V3b.6.2 (W MEDAUVILLE) A/79 Q26A, C/79 Q26B with forward section at Q27b.5.2. B/79 V6d, D/79 V6a. Registrations checked. Day firing about 50 rounds per battery m, harassing and including Crab RES. Night harassing fire about 130 rounds per Battery	MW

WAR DIARY
or
INTELLIGENCE SUMMARY.

(Erase heading not required.)

Army Form C. 2118.

Instructions regarding War Diaries and Intelligence Summaries are contained in F. S. Regs., Part II. and the Staff Manual respectively. Title pages will be prepared in manuscript.

Place	Date 1918	Hour	Summary of Events and Information	Remarks and references to Appendices
ENGELBELMER	April 26		Normal harassing fire by day and night.	
	27		79th Bde, 3/159 and 112th Siege Battery (5-inch Hows.) bombarded Strong Point in A.15.b.4 WOOD (WWR 3.1) from 12.30 pm to 9.40 pm. together with neighbouring trenches MG posts etc, preparatory to occupation of the point WWR 3.1 by the 17th Royal Scots (156.9 Bde.) at 9.40 pm.	MS
		9.40pm	Two SOS signals observed on Left Battalion front. All Batteries opened up on SOS targets. No infantry action developed, beyond enemy patrol in No mans land.	MS
			Minor operation timed for 9.40 pm cancelled.	MS
	28		Normal harassing fire by day & night. Enemy very quiet, using shells	MS
	29		do do	
	30		do do	

Inverarrn
Lieut Col. 79th
Commanding 79th Bde RFA

WAR DIARY
INTELLIGENCE SUMMARY.
(Erase heading not required.)

Army Form C. 2118.

Place	Date	Hour	Summary of Events and Information	Remarks and references to Appendices
		I	APPENDIX. Ammunition Expenditure April 1918. 9129 A 7154 Ay 3882 By 262 BNC	
		II	Casualties - Killed Officers 2 OR 2 Wounded Officers 7 OR 26 Wounded (Gas) Officers 4 OR 54	
		III	Wastage from Sickness. Officers 1 OR 24	
		IV	Home Casualties - Killed 15 Destroyed 4 Evacuated 49 (T M V S)	

J Warren
Lieut Col RFA
CmDg. 79th FaB

30 April 1918.

Vol 34

Army Form C. 2118.

79 Bde R.F.A.

WAR DIARY
or
INTELLIGENCE SUMMARY

(Erase heading not required.)

79 Bde R.F.A.

Place	Date 1918	Hour	Summary of Events and Information	Remarks and references to Appendices
ENGELBELMER	May 1		Bde in action. Hqrs. in HEDAUVILLE. V3b 6.2	
			A/79 Q26a	
			B/79 V6d	
			C/79 Q26a	
			D/79 V6a	
	2		50% of guns silent except in case of SOS — all firing from forward positions	MM
	3		Harassing fire by day, night on river crossings, roads, tracks	
	4		Usual harassing fire carried out. Visibility low. 35th Division Relief by 38th (Welsh) Division complete on night 3/4th May	MMS
		10pm	One Section of 79th Bde Batteries relieved by 157 Bde RFA (35 DA) and taken into action in relief of sections of 223 Army Brigade, covering the Brigade of the Division on the North (17½ Div.) MESNIL SECTOR	MMS
MESNIL	5	10pm	Relief of 223 Bde by 79th Bde Complete. Hqrs at P24c.o.o	
			A/79 4 guns (Silent) P30d4.2, 2 guns (active) Q3;b 6.4. B/79 V65 8.9.09	
			B guns all silent. C/79 4 guns (Silent) P36d 8.7, 2 guns (active) Q32d 2.9	MMS
			D/79 4 How (Silent) P2H c 8.4 2 Hows (active) Q25d 9.2 (Catapult D/79 transferred to R)	
	6		Sector from Jeatnuse to Nyestekin Copse.	
	7		79th RFA covered 57th R.I. 17th Division	
	8		And harassing fire day & night from guns & howrs not from the pit.	M2.

Army Form C. 2118.

WAR DIARY
or
INTELLIGENCE SUMMARY.
(Erase heading not required.)

Place	Date	Hour	Summary of Events and Information	Remarks and references to Appendices
MESNIL	May 9		Quiet day - from Intercepts, 63rd Div. relieves 17th Div. (189 Bde relieves 87th)	6(a)
	10.	9.15 am	38th Division carried out an attack on the high ground in Aveluy Wood. 79 A Bde took part in its execution. Attack was unsuccessful owing to enemy M.Gs fire & the close nature of own barrage.	
			Situation normal, kept fire heavily concentrated on MESNIL.	6(b)
			ENGELBELMER and BULLINS portion at night. Crucifix alright in billeting area.	
			79 Bde carries out harassed harassing fire on bridges, trenches	
	11			
	12		Enemy defence rather feeble. Ammunition expended: 300 rounds per 18 Pr per night expended	6(c)
	13		by 79/29 trench mortars, 10 rounds shelled: no casualties.	
	14			
	15			
	16		Casualties: officer - Lieut. J.F. STRONG killed at B/79 from hostile (B/79) mostly shrapnel in from puits. 9/5 E.F. ROBSON severely wounded	
	17		since has died of wounds.	
	18			
	19.	12.15 am	HOSTILE Bth 189 Bde Can carried over unsuccessful raid on the 78th Bde position (near HAMEL) 79 & 14 Bde supplied covering fire heavily on the Run/MICRE Run to Divisional 79/19 Bde took less a standing barrage on Kuvalla & harasser the Rt. of t.	6(d)
			Ruth Jrnes WYPRA. 50 hour & 1 persons & known rite held.	
			On casualties.	

WAR DIARY
or
INTELLIGENCE SUMMARY

Army Form C. 2118.

Place	Date	Hour	Summary of Events and Information	Remarks and references to Appendices
MESNIL	20	1 Am	1 Section from R85 relieved by 1 section from R85 223rd Bn RFA (63rd Div)	W92
		10 Pm	Relief of 79th by 227th Bde complete. 79th Bde withdrawn & began move at TOUTENCOURT.	
	21		C. Bn resting in began lines. 2i/c HARPONVILLE — VARIENNES Rd.	
	22		Snr in Camps Rest Reserve. HQ at TOUTENCOURT.	
	23		From 6-8 Am daily Bde under 1 hours notice to move.	W92
	24		Enemy attack expected (from premium statement)	
	25		1 Section from R85 relieves one section from R85 of 232nd Army Bde.	
			17th Div'n by Left Division of V Corps.	
			Covering (17th Div) relieved 12th Div.	
26.	8 pm	Completion of Relief. J 232 Rn by 79th Bn.	W92
			79 Bn in return on "Clark" Bn covering 17th Div'n (50th Bde) P.10.C.8520.	
27.			Locations as follows:- HQ (East of ACHEUX WOOD)	
			A/79. P 12 c 1025.	
			B/79. P 12 c 1580.	
			C/79. P 11 c 8050.	
			D/79. P 5 d 1030. (BEAUSSART)	
BEAUSSART 27-			Bde HQ moved to LOUVENCOURT	

WAR DIARY
INTELLIGENCE SUMMARY

Army Form C. 2118.

Place	Date	Hour	Summary of Events and Information	Remarks and references to Appendices
BEAUSSART	28		Bde silent: Quiet day. Batteries sound strength.	Appx
	29	12 noon	Bde took over from 62nd Bde (12 D.A.) and became the Left "Active" Bde covering 58th Inf Bde. Bde HQ with 58th Inf Bde at MAILLY (P.12.b.90.70) C/75 moved to Q.1.a.80.70 (north of MAILLY) relieving C/62 D/75 " Q.7.d.90.30 (East of MAILLY) relieving D/63. A & B batteries remained in same positions. Reputation carried out. Casualties 2 O.R. C/75 killed + 2 O.R. wounded (HQ)	Appx
MAILLY-MAILLET	30		Hyperon harassing fire carried out at night.	
	31		+ harassing enemy approaches during the day. Task carried out at set points + new HQ under construction near BEAUSSART	Appx

W.H. Hampton
Capt. RA
79 Bde RFA.

Army Form C. 2118.

WAR DIARY
or
79th Bde R.F.A. INTELLIGENCE SUMMARY. May 1918

(Erase heading not required.)

Place	Date	Hour	Summary of Events and Information	Remarks and references to Appendices
		I	Annual Expenditure May 1918 (Approx.) A¹. 7000 A.X. 4000 B X 3000 13 N.C. 500.	
		II	Casualties. Killed. Officers. 2 O.R. 4 Wounded (Officers.) M.C. O.R. 12 Wounded (gassed) O.R. 25.	
		III	Wastage from Sickness. Officers 1 O.R. 24.	
		IV	Horse Casualties. Killed 1 Destroyed 1 Died 1 Evacuated to A.V.S. 26.	

W.A. Huntrods
Capt + Adjt
79 Bde R.F.A.

WAR DIARY

79 TMB INTELLIGENCE SUMMARY. JUNE.

Place	Date	Hour	Summary of Events and Information	Remarks and references to Appendices
MAILLY-MAILLET	1.		Batteries in action as at the end of May. i.e. Bde Hd. with 51st (Left) Div. Bde Hd. at P.12.b.9070. MAILLY. A/79 2 guns (action) P.12.c.06.20 1 gun (silent) P.11.B.70.70 ⎫ BEAUSSART B/79 4 guns P.12.c.15.70 ⎬ BEAUSSART C/79 6 guns Q.1.a.80.80 ⎭ In MAILLY D/79 6 hows Q.7.d.90.30 East of MAILLY. — concentration in conjunction with Corps Heavy Artillery.	6/1
	2. 3. 4. 5. 6. 7.		Harassing fire every night. Several successful shots on enemy transport and horses. 5th & 6th enemy shelled battery positions heavily with 4.2 and 5.9 Hows, but inflicted no casualties; 3 guns put out of action, which from Corps made Remarks. New Bde H.Qrs. near BEAUSSART when construction. Reputation carried out for raid by 50 Bde.	6/2 6/3
	8.	10.5pm	Zero. Barrage good & raid very successful. 30 prisoners and 4 MGs taken.	MMB.

Army Form C. 2118.

WAR DIARY
or
INTELLIGENCE SUMMARY.
(Erase heading not required.)

Instructions regarding War Diaries and Intelligence Summaries are contained in F. S. Regs., Part II. and the Staff Manual respectively. Title pages will be prepared in manuscript.

Place	Date	Hour	Summary of Events and Information	Remarks and references to Appendices
MAILLY MAILLET	June 9		Usual harassing fire & registration forward on nights 9/12.	MW
	10			
	11	10.55 pm	Zero hour for raid by 35th Division (Division on Right). 79th Brigade forming flank barrage. Raid successful & reached slight.	MW
	12.	3 pm	4.5 hows and 6" hows bombarded enemy TMs and defences for 30 minutes, 18 Pdrs also sweeping the area.	M.
	13			
	14			
	15		Usual harassing fire by day & night - Enemy fire and	MW
	16		activity normal.	
	17			
	18	midnight	42nd Division carried out a raid on left. 79th Bde firing a flank barrage on SOS lines.	MW.
	19.		Usual harassing fire by night & day.	MW
	~~20~~	10 pm	Gas bombardment by Corps 6" hows v 4.5 hows, for 3 hours	MW
	20	9.50pm	Gas bombardment repeated. Usual harassing fire.	MW.
	21			
	22		Usual harassing fire night & day. Enemy very quiet	MW

WAR DIARY
INTELLIGENCE SUMMARY.

Army Form C. 2118.

Place	Date	Hour	Summary of Events and Information	Remarks and references to Appendices
MAILLY-MAILLET	June 23.		Usual harassing fire. Relief of 17th Div. (Divl. Arty) by 63rd Div. Divl. Arty.	MM
	24.		One section per Battery relieved by section 1/63rd RN DA.	MM
	25.	8.30 am	Relief of 17th DA by 63rd DA completed. 79th Bde in wagon lines near TOUTENCOURT in GHQ Reserve at 1hrs notice to move from midnight. At 5am, 9 hrs notice to midnight M.	MM
TOUTENCOURT				MM
	26.	10 am	Brigade moved to wagon lines between villages near EAN[?] ACHEUX and CLAIREFAYE. Places of assembly and positions for various lines of defence reconnoitred.	MM
LEALVILLERS				MM
	27		} Brigade resting and refitting.	MM
	28			
	29			
	30	8.30pm	Brigade moved to Wagon lines between PONT NOYELLES and DAOURS in 4th Australian Divisional Area - South Army. March commenced at 8.30pm and new Wagon lines were reached by	Jm

Army Form C. 2118.

WAR DIARY
or
INTELLIGENCE SUMMARY.
(Erase heading not required.)

Instructions regarding War Diaries and Intelligence
Summaries are contained in F. S. Regs., Part II.
and the Staff Manual respectively. Title pages
will be prepared in manuscript.

Place	Date	Hour	Summary of Events and Information	Remarks and references to Appendices
LEALVILLERS	30	3. a.m 1st July.	One OR was wounded by bomb from enemy aircraft en route	Jm

Swarren
Lieut. Col. R.F.A.
Commanding 79th Bde R.F.A.

Army Form C. 2118.

WAR DIARY
or
INTELLIGENCE SUMMARY
(Erase heading not required.)

79th F.A.B. June 1918

APPENDIX

I. Amm.n. Expended A 12872 AX 5093 BX 5986 Chemical 1344
                                                Smoke 92.

II. Casualties. Killed   Officers Nil   OR Nil
                 Wounded   "   Nil   " 34
                 " (Gassed)   "   Nil   "   2

III. Wastage from Sickness Officers Nil   OR 31.

IV. Horse Casualties. Died 1
                       Totals 40.

Lieut Col RFA
Cmdg 79th F.A.B.

30 June 1918.

Army Form C. 2118.

WAR DIARY
or
INTELLIGENCE SUMMARY.
(Erase heading not required.)

79th 7 A.B.

Vol 36

Instructions regarding War Diaries and Intelligence Summaries are contained in F. S. Regs., Part II. and the Staff Manual respectively. Title pages will be prepared in manuscript.

Place	Date 1916	Hour	Summary of Events and Information	Remarks and references to Appendices
BUSSY-LES-DAOURS	JULY 1.	11.30am	Bde. and Bty. Commanders reconnoitred new battery positions near HAMLET. Brigade is under the orders of Right Group Australian Field Artillery (Lt.Col. T.I.C. Williams D.S.O.)	(I.35.c.30.20.)
		9.50.	Brigade took up positions near HAMLET. HQs at N. edge of CORBIE. First echelon of ammunition brought up to guns and waggon lines unloaded by ho.1. Sections. 17th D.A.C.	
HAMLET	2		Consolidating positions and getting up ammunition. Guns are camouflaged in open positions. Care taken to show no movement or signs of activity. No registration is allowed.	A/79. O.6.d. 53.20 B/79. O.6.b. 80.95 C/79. O.6.b. 90.90 D/79. O.6.d. 84.42
	3		"Y" Day [crossed out] on boot hunt.	
	4	3.10am	Attacked [crossed out] Australian Infantry composed of 3 Australian Bdes. one United States Battalion. Bde. put down supporting barrage with received number of smoke shell to assist tanks to mark "half time" etc... All objectives taken including village of HAMEL. Prisoners 1350, M.Gs. 90, T.Ms. 2 etc.	
		10pm 10.20pm	Enemy Counter-attacked on Bde. front. attack repulsed + 50 prisoners taken.	

Army Form C. 2118.

WAR DIARY
or
INTELLIGENCE SUMMARY

(Erase heading not required.)

79th J.A.B.

Place	Date July 1918	Hour	Summary of Events and Information	Remarks and references to Appendices
HAMELET DAOURS	5	9 pm	Bde. commenced to pull out of Positions.	
	6		Brigade marched to LEALVILLERS to Puvino Wagon Lines in O. 24. Many cases of influenza have developed.	A/79 14 crows D/79 16
LEALVILLERS	7		Brigade being now in the N. Brigade of the Artillery of the R. supporting Division V Corps. moved to "Practice Assembly Positions" near HARPONVILLE. Positions reached 3 hours 20 mins from time of receipt of order. Returned to Wagon Lines at 5-30 am	
	8			
	9		Brigade resting & refitting. 30 more cases of influenza, including 2/Lt. DRIVER. 2/LIEUT H.W. GORDON and LIEUT W.A. CARNE rejoined.	
	10			
	11			
	12		Brigade rejoined 62nd Bde. R.F.A. (12th Div Arty.) in the line at short notice.	
MARTINSART	13	2 am	Relief completed. Hdqrs. near HEDAUVILLE V.3.d 6.7. All harassing fire done by forward guns. Remainder of Bty. silent. Harassing fire day & night on bridges over ANCRE.	A/79 5"gun. V.10.a. 92.67 19m. V.6.c. 99.39 13pm. Tank Gun W.1.b. 80.05 B/79 5"gun. V.10.c. 30.35 19m. V.17.b. 90.60 C/79 4.5 How. P.28.d.10.16 19m. Q.26.c.07.92 Tank Gun. W.1.b. 80.50 D/79 5"gun P.29.c. 50.05 19m. V.6.a. 81.78

Army Form C. 2118.

WAR DIARY
or
INTELLIGENCE SUMMARY.
(Erase heading not required.)

79th Bde R.F.A.

Place	Date July	Hour	Summary of Events and Information	Remarks and references to Appendices
MARTINSART	14 15 16 17		Usual harassing fire, chiefly on bridges and approaches. Average expenditure 18 pdr. 1000 rds. 4.5" How. 330 rds. daily.	Yh.
	18		"C" & "D" Batteries' Positions brought within Div. area from outlying points. Advanced guns of 18 pdrs. Btys formed into one half Bty. New Positions as follows:—	
			"C" Bty. (4 guns) V. t. c. 35. 45"	
			(1 gun) V. b. c. 98. 60	
			"D" Bty. (4 guns) V. b. a. 82. 78	
			"B" Bty. (2 guns) V. b. c. 80. 45	
			(1 gun) V. b. c. 90. 50	
	19 20 21 22 23		Usual harassing fire, and registration.	Yh.
	24 25 26 27 28 29		Harassing fire on approaches and occupied areas & wirecutting.	fr.
	30		Co-operated with Corps Artillery in half hour intense bombardment of selected areas in enemy's front & support systems.	fr.
	31		Usual harassing fire. [signature]	fr.

1st August 1918. Cmdg. 79 Bde. R.F.A.

Army Form C. 2118.

WAR DIARY
or
INTELLIGENCE SUMMARY.

79th T.A.B.   JULY 1918

Place	Date	Hour	Summary of Events and Information APPENDIX	Remarks and references to Appendices
MARTINSART	JULY			
		I	Amm. Expended A 14040 AX 8,348 AS 446	
			BX 7,245 GAS 728 BS 99	
		II	Casualties Killed Officers NIL O.R. 3	
			Wounded " NIL " 1	
			" (gassed) " NIL " NIL	
		III	Wastage from Sickness Officers 1 O.R. 177	
		IV	Horse Casualties Died 1	
			To M.V.S. 52 horses	
			8 mules	

Sugaren
Lt. Col. R.F.A.
Cmdg. 79th Bde. R.F.A.

1st August 1918.

17th Divl.
Artillery

79th BRIGADE,

ROYAL FIELD ARTILLERY,

AUGUST 1918.

Army Form C. 2118.

WAR DIARY
or
INTELLIGENCE SUMMARY.
(Erase heading not required.)

79 Bde. R.F.A.

WD 37

Place	Date August	Hour	Summary of Events and Information	Remarks and references to Appendices
MARTINSART	1	9.10pm	50th Infy. Bde. raided enemy front again, taking 16 prisoners & 4 M.G's. Bde. participated in the barrage.	—
	2	1-30am	51st Infy. Bde. raided enemy posts & found front line evacuated. Enemy retreated E. of River ANCRE on whole of Divison front.	—
	3		Usual harassing fire on new enemy posts. T.M's. approached the hostile fire below normal.	—
	4			—
	5			—
	6		Bde. pulled out of action. Two Bty's. relieved by batteries of 38th D.A. At wagon lines near CONTAY. Bde. HQ. at TOUTENCOURT.	—
TOUTENCOURT	7			—
	8		Bde. — (inc G.H.Q. Reserve) moved to Area near BLANGY-TRONVILLE under Australian Corps. 4th Army.	—
BLANGY-TRONVILLE	9		Moved to area on N.E outskirts of CORBIE.	—
CORBIE	10		Brigade reading & refitting.	—
	11		Major W.E. Thompson C/79. to hospital with ditto. in order appendicitis.	—
PROYART	12		Relieved 8th Aust. Bde. D.A. in daylight — completed relief 9 p.m. HQ. Q.u.a. 70.20 Batteries in Q.21. Crossing 51st Infy Bde. with 78th Bde. R.F.A. Col. Warren in command of Group.	—

24

Army Form C. 2118.

WAR DIARY
or
INTELLIGENCE SUMMARY.

79 Bde. R.F.A.

Place	Date	Hour	Summary of Events and Information	Remarks and references to Appendices
PROYART	13		All batteries moved forward to positions as follows:— A/79. Q.9.d.8.5" B/79. Q.17.b.3.6 C/79. Q.8.d.0.4 D/79. Q.1.d.5.5. Group HQ. with 57th Infy. Bde. HQ. at MORCOURT.	
	14		Quiet day. Harassing fire on Vallies behind enemy lines.	Ja
	15		Naval Harassing fire.	Ja
	16		Consolidating.	Ja
BUSSY-LES-DAOURS	17		Relieved by 5th Aust. Divl. Arty. (14th Bde.). 79th Bde. to VECQUEMONT area. HQ Bussy-Les-Daours.	Ja
	18		Resting and refitting.	
TOUTENCOURT	19		Bde. marched to old wagon lines near CONTAY. HQ at TOUTENCOURT	Ja
MESNIL	20		Into action at dusk in MESNIL VALLEY. Ammn. taken up.	Ja
	21		Batteries Participated in attack on ANCRE defences. LIEUT A.E. IMPEY	Ja
	22		Rejoined	
	23		Ditto. HQ to old Battn. HQ. near AUCHONVILLERS	Ja
THIEPVAL	24		Barrage fired to assist attack by 17th Div. Attack Successful. Bde. occupied Ruins. ANCRE during morning and came into action between THIEPVAL and POZIERES. Good work done by Forward observation officers 2/LIEUT F.M. MEDHURST & LIEUT F.M. MEDHURST & attached to Battalion single guns attached to	Ja

Army Form C. 2118.

WAR DIARY
or
INTELLIGENCE SUMMARY.

(Erase heading not required.)

70 Bde. R.F.A.

Instructions regarding War Diaries and Intelligence Summaries are contained in F. S. Regs., Part II. and the Staff Manual respectively. Title pages will be prepared in manuscript.

Place	Date	Hour	Summary of Events and Information	Remarks and references to Appendices
COURCELLETTE	25		Advance continued. Bde. moved to position E. of COURCELLETTE. Water scarcity - needed supply River ANCRE. Enemy counter attack repulsed.	on
MARTINPUICH	26		Advance continued. Batteries near MARTINPUICH. HQ between MARTINPUICH and BAPAUME-ALBERT Rd.	on
	27 28		Batteries near MARTINPUICH. HQ unchanged. Minor engagements and small frequent consolidating.	on
FLERS	29		Advance continued. Batteries to Valley W. of GUEDECOURT. HQ in FLERS Valley. Single guns forward engaged movement successfully. CAPT. C.D. MORGAN and 2/Lt J.S.W. MOORE wounded.	on
	30 31		Small operations + attacks carried out to gain tactical points. Bde. supported 17th Div. Infy. and 38th Div. Infy. in these efforts.	on

[signature] Lt. Col. R.F.A.
Cmdg 70 F.A.B.

4th Sept 1918.

Army Form C. 2118.

WAR DIARY
or
INTELLIGENCE SUMMARY.
(Erase heading not required.)

79 Bde R.F.A.   AUGUST 1918

Place	Date Aug	Hour	Summary of Events and Information	Remarks and references to Appendices
		I	Ammn. Expended. A 10,109 AX 8,169 AS 3,109 (approx) BX 6,719 GAS 300 BS 1006	
		II	Casualties Killed Officers NIL O.R. NIL	
			Wounded " 4 O.R. 9	
			Gassed " 1 O.R. 2	
			Accidentally injured " 1 O.R. 2	
		III	Wastage from sickness " 3 O.R. 39	
		IV	Horse Casualties Died NIL	
			Killed 1 horse	
			Wounded 1 horse	
			TO M.V.S. 28 horses	
			4 mules	
			4th Sept 1918 [signature] Lt Col RFA	
			Comd. 79 Bde.	

Army Form C. 2118.

WAR DIARY
or
INTELLIGENCE SUMMARY.
(Erase heading not required)

79-Bde. R.F.A.   Vol 38

Place	Date	Hour	Summary of Events and Information	Remarks and references to Appendices
FLERS	SEPT. 1		Consolidating and bringing up ammn.	App.
	2		Supported attack on LE TRANSLOY. Attack succeeded in outflanking LE TRANSLOY from the North.	App.
BUS	3		Enemy retired and was followed up by us to YTRES – EQUANCOURT line. Batteries with forward guns and sections engaged movement on several occasions.	App.
	4		Heavy hostile shelling of battery and magazine areas – chiefly instantaneous H.E. mixed with gas (Blue Cross). Captain H.W. Gordon M.C. wounded and 8. O.R. including Sergt. Chapman h.m. Bde. Sig. Sect. Bde. assisted with barrages.	App.
	5		Local attacks carried out. Bde. assisted with barrages.	App.
LECHELLE	6		Advance continued. Batteries moved forward to valley E. of Canal du Nord between YTRES and EQUANCOURT. H.Q. between four Winds Farm and Canal. Infy. held line of FINS Ridge.	App.
FINS	7		Advance continued. Infy. to Junch Ayclin. DESSART RIDGE. Batteries and H.Q./79 one mile due North of FINS. Battalion guns and forward sections engaged movement.	App.
	8		Consolidating	App.
	9		Attack in early morning, partially successful; Capture enemy breeze trench protective barrage against enemy counter attack.	App.

Army Form C. 2118.

WAR DIARY
or
INTELLIGENCE SUMMARY.

Instructions regarding War Diaries and Intelligence Summaries are contained in F.S. Regs., Part II. and the Staff Manual respectively. Title pages will be prepared in manuscript.

70th Bde. R. Fus. *(Erase heading not required.)*

Place	Date SEPT	Hour	Summary of Events and Information	Remarks and references to Appendices
~~PIERS~~ FINS.	10		After mk night, attack to gain remainder of objective (which again W. of GOUZEAUCOURT) postponed. Artillery bombarded but no Infty. action. Bde. until tactical control of 38th D.A.	Jm
	11		Consolidating. 17th Durh. Infy. relieved.	Jm
	12		Quiet days. Usual harassing fire on enemy trench Rds & trenches.	Jm
	13			Jm
	14			
	15		— do —	MW
	16			
	17	a.m.		
	18	5.20	I Corps attacked pivoting on GOUZEAUCOURT. GAUCHE WOOD captured by 17th Div. All objectives attained except trenches west of Gouzeaucourt, where 38 Div. met strong opposition from JAEGERS and were unable to take AFRICAN TRENCH which not running, with further heavy barrages.	MW
	19		Quiet days. Usual harassing fire on roads & communications	MW
	20			
	21			
	22			
	23			
	24			
	25			

Army Form C. 2118.

WAR DIARY
or
INTELLIGENCE SUMMARY.
(Erase heading not required.)

Instructions regarding War Diaries and Intelligence Summaries are contained in F. S. Regs., Part II. and the Staff Manual respectively. Title pages will be prepared in manuscript.

Place	Date 1918	Hour	Summary of Events and Information	Remarks and references to Appendices
FINS.	26		Preparing for attack on 27th. Forward positions reconnoitred and ammn dumped.	
	27th	5.20 am	IV Corps & VII Corps attacked, pushing on GOUZEAUCOURT. Attack complete success except on extreme right, where little progress was made. (Regt of 5th Div. Front.)	MN
		7.52 am	62nd Bde (21 Div) captured remainder of AFRICAN TRENCH. 10 Corps Boundary. Lost by counter attack about 6.30 pm. Small party of enemy penetrated to within 300 yards of Bde Forward Positions.	MN
	28	9 am	Forward move was postponed. Infy (62 Bde) reestablished themselves in AFRICAN Trench, and pushed out patrols N. of GOUZEAUCOURT. About midday batteries moved forward to Q34. Enemy reported clear of GOUZEAUCOURT.	MN
GOUZEAUCOURT WOOD	29		At 3.20 am & 5.30 am Barrages were fired in support of operation to capture trenches in R32 & X3. This was unsuccessful. Later in the day enemy evacuated these trenches & Bttys moved up to Q36 & W6d. B. HQ. moved to Q36 c	W.F.S.
VILLERS-GUISLAINE	30		Enemy evacuated VILLERS-GUISLAINE and GONNELIEU and trenches in R35 & X5. Bttys & H.Q. moved to X3.	W.F.S.

Army Form C. 2118.

WAR DIARY
or
INTELLIGENCE SUMMARY.
(Erase heading not required.)

79th F.A.B.   SEPTEMBER 1918

Instructions regarding War Diaries and Intelligence Summaries are contained in F. S. Regs., Part II. and the Staff Manual respectively. Title pages will be prepared in manuscript.

Place	Date SEPT.	Hour	Summary of Events and Information	Remarks and references to Appendices
VILLERS- GUISLAIN			APPENDIX	
		I	Ammn. Expended (approx) A.17,904. AX.18,402. AS.396. BX.8511. BCG.378. BNC.560. BSS.852.	
		II	Casualties Killed Officers NIL O.R 1 Wounded " 3 " 22 Gassed " 1 " 4	
		III	Wastage from Sickers " NIL " 30	
		IV	Horse Casualties Died NIL Killed 19 horses 8 mules Wounded NIL To M.V.S. 56 horses 8 mules	

4th Oct 1918
[signature] Major R.F.A. for Lt.Col. R.F.A.
Cmdg. 79th F.A.B.

WAR DIARY or INTELLIGENCE SUMMARY

Army Form C. 2118.

79th F.A.B.

Vol. 39

Place	Date 1918	Hour	Summary of Events and Information	Remarks and references to Appendices
VILLERS-GUISLAINE	Oct. 1.		Quiet day. Enemy evacuated country W. of CANAL DE ST. QUENTIN on Divisional front.	W.T.S.
	2.		Quiet day. Usual harassing fire on enemy Sunken Rds & trenches.	W.T.S.
	3. } 4. }		do.	W.T.S.
	5.		Enemy evacuated HINDENBURG LINE. Our infantry crossed CANAL & occupied HINDENBURG SUPPORT. Patrols pushed forward to keep in touch with enemy. Bttys & H.Q. moved to X.4.d. During the night C/79 moved across the CANAL to S.2.e.	W.T.S.
HONNECOURT	6.		Enemy holding BEAUREVOIR LINE. Our Infantry (64th Bde) established themselves in SUNKEN ROAD running between BONNE ENFANT FARM and MONTECOUVEZ FARM thence along ROAD to T.1.b.5.2. H.Q. moved to S.5.a.1.2. Bttys moved to positions as follows:- A/79 S.6.a.4.9 B/79 M.34.d.9.3 C/79 S.11.b.3.7 D/79 S.5.a.3.6.	W.T.S.
	7.		Quiet day. Usual harassing fire on enemy Sunken Rds & trenches.	W.T.S.

Army Form C. 2118.

WAR DIARY
or
INTELLIGENCE SUMMARY.
(Erase heading not required.)

79th F.A.B.

Instructions regarding War Diaries and Intelligence Summaries are contained in F. S. Regs., Part II. and the Staff Manual respectively. Title pages will be prepared in manuscript.

Place	Date	Hour	Summary of Events and Information	Remarks and references to Appendices
MALASSISE COPSE	8	01—	64th + 110th Bdes (21st Div) attacked. The objective which was ANGLES CHATEAU and line of the road to N33a0.7 was obtained. This was supported by 78th, 79th and 94th Bdes R.F.A.	
		05.15	The 110th Bde attacked from the line of trenches N33a0.7 — N32a0.8 and gained the objective N21a8.8 — N20b6.8 — N20b6.3 — N19d4.7. This was supported by 78th, 79th & 94th Bde R.F.A.	W.F.S.
		0800	62nd Bde. attached from line HAUTE FARM — HEUTEBISE FARM. The objective was WALINCOURT and high ground in N18a. This was obtained at dusk. During the 3rd attack the Batteries moved to positions in N20c1and N26b. H.Q. established at N20d 6.5.	
CAULLERY.	9.	0500.	17th Div. took over from 21st Div. Enemy evacuated SELVIGNY and CAULLERY. 51st Infan. Bde. came in touch with enemy on Western outskirts of MONTIGNY. Batteries moved to positions in O15b&d. B.H.Q established in CAULLERY.	W.F.S.
INCHY	10		Advance continued. Bde. Passed through MONTIGNY. AUDENCOURT and INCHY in support of 50th Infy. Bde. Enemy had evacuated. Touch was regained in vicinity of NEUVILLY. Many civilians in village captured. Bty's took up positions in J. 23 B. Forward Gun D.H.Q. J. 18 and effectively made to engage movement & silence enemy batteries, two bty here heavily shelled from L. flank MAJOR V.N. MACKENZIE M.C. W.T. B.M.Q. SE INCHY.	

Army Form C. 2118.

WAR DIARY
or
INTELLIGENCE SUMMARY.

(Erase heading not required.)

79th Bde RFA

1918

Place	Date	Hour	Summary of Events and Information	Remarks and references to Appendices
INCHY	11		Consolidating. Our hostile fire, the left flank having been cleared up	gh
	12		52nd Infy. Bde. attacked to gain village of NEUVILLY and high ground beyond. Attack partially successful, enemy reinforced counter attacked. Our troops finally held line of river SELLE, afterwards being consolidated.	
	13			
	14		Consolidating. Harassing fire carried out on enemy positions, enemy made but little reply.	gh
	15			
	16			
	17		During night Bty's moved forward to valley in V.18, a without evacuating any casualties.	gh
	18		Consolidating new positions. Registering.	gh
	19		Consolidating. Quiet - enemy retaliation with Det. Arty - a enemy bombs maintain desultory interest throughout day. 2/Lieut E.W. KING MASTR & L. WILLMOTT slightly wounded.	gh
			2/Lieut E.W. KING severely wounded.	gh
	20		Attack at 2.a.m by 51st Infy. Bde. High Ground E. of NEUVILLY and village of AMERVAL. 2/Lieut E.W. KING died of wounds at c.c.s.	gh
NEUVILLY	21		Bde. moved forward to positions E. of NEUVILLY. Three casualties.	gh
	22		Quiet. Consolidating positions + getting up ammn.	gh

WAR DIARY
INTELLIGENCE SUMMARY

1918 70 Bde RFA

Place	Date	Hour	Summary of Events and Information	Remarks and references to Appendices
NEUVILLY	Oct 23		Attack at 2 a.m. by 21st Division was successful. Bde. moved forward to position E.1 OVILLERS. Div. HQ at OVILLERS.	ap
VENDEGIES-AU-BOIS	24		Attack continued. Batteries moved to E.1 VENDEGIES-AU-BOIS. 2/Lieut HABBIJOE KNIGHT sick. Quit duty. Evacuated.	ap
	25			ap
	26		Bde pulled out of action for short rest to CLARY.	ap
CLARY	27			ap
	28		Bde resting and refitting. Major H.F. WILLMOT returned from hospital. 2/Lieut D.M. EDINGTON joined.	ap
	29			ap
	30		Returned to position vacated on 26th inst. S.O.S. lines taken up by 12-30 a.m. 31st inst.	ap
VENDEGIES-AU-BOIS	31		Registration shooting fair carried out. New position further forward reconnoitred.	ap

W Walker
Major RFA
Cmdg 70th Bde RFA

1/11/18

WAR DIARY or INTELLIGENCE SUMMARY

70th Bde. R.F.A. October 1918

Place	Hour Date 19th	Summary of Events and Information	Remarks and references to Appendices
Oct 1		APPENDIX	
		I. Ammn. Refunded A 18,000 AX 6,000 AS 500 AT 24	
		(approx) BX 9,000 BS 200	
		II. Casualties Killed Officers 1 O.R. 6	
		Wounded " 1 " 33	
		Gassed " NIL " 1	
		III. Wastage from Sickness Officers 5 O.R. 90	
		(inc 3 died)	
		IV. Horse Casualties Killed 17	
		Died 2	
		To M.V.S. 58	
		Wavell Major R.F.A.	
		1/11/18 Cmdg 70th Bde. R.F.A.	

Army Form C. 2118.

WAR DIARY
or
INTELLIGENCE SUMMARY.
(Erase heading not required.)

70th Bde R.F.A. November 1918

Instructions regarding War Diaries and Intelligence Summaries are contained in F. S. Regs., Part II. and the Staff Manual respectively. Title pages will be prepared in manuscript.

Place	Date	Hour	Summary of Events and Information	Remarks and references to Appendices
VENDEGIES AU-BOIS	1		① Quiet day	
	2		Major W.H. Mackenzie M.C. rejoined. Ammn. taken up to forward positions.	
POIX-DU-NORD	3		HQ moved to POIX-DU-NORD. Batteries moved to forward position N. of POIX-DU-NORD in readiness for attack.	
	4	5:30am	Attack on our Army fronts. Brigade fired outpost barrage during which one D.R. killed and 14 D.R. wounded. Lieut W.D. MATHIESON wounded.	
FUTOY		11 am	Batteries moved to positions near FUTOY W. of FORET DE MORMAL. On O.P. killed and 10 O.R. wounded on Rd. HQ en route by aeroplane bombs. Batteries fired concentrations on points of resistance & roads in FORET DE MORMAL to assist advance. Advance carried out by 5DD, 51st & 50th Infty Bde. in order named. One line at night near immediately W. of LOCQUIGNOL	
	5		Advance continued in wet weather. Batteries came into action at TETE NOIR after overcoming transport difficulties on roads through FORET DE MORMAL owing to trees ordered. One line at end of day along W. bank of SAMBRE River through BERLAIMONT. Wgn lines lat LOCQUIGNOL Ram ordered. Inft'y. pushed across River SAMBRE during night.	
TETE NOIR	6		Batteries moved to E. of TETE NOIR	

Army Form C. 2118.

WAR DIARY
or
INTELLIGENCE SUMMARY.
(Erase heading not required.)

79th Bde R.F.A. NOV. 18

Place	Date	Hour	Summary of Events and Information	Remarks and references to Appendices
BACHANT	7		The Brigade crossed the River Sambre at BACHANT. Batteries in action W. of BACHANT, advancing as far as BACHANT by noon. HQ in BACHANT. Considerable shelling during the day, but Infty. Bde. held up E. of LIMONT FONTAINE	JW
	8		17th Divl. Infty. relieved 21st Divl. Infty. in line. Batteries moved E. of BACHANT.	JW
		(4.45pm) (6.45pm)	Divl. Infty. to assist Infty. to Captain Ribm time (MAUBEUGE - AVESNES Rd)	
LIMONT-FONTAINE	9		Orders received not to move further forward. Cavalry Patrols pushed out to keep touch with enemy. HQ to LIMONT FONTAINE	JW
	10		Wagon lines joined Gun lines. Waiting for further instructions	JW
	11	11.00	Hostilities ceased at 11.00 hours. Orders received to G.O.C. ...	JW
	12		Resting & refitting at LIMONT-FONTAINE	JW
ENGLE FONTAINE	13	10.00	Bde. moved back to ENGLE FONTAINE	JW
CLARY	14		Continued march to CLARY	JW
ESNES	15		marched to ESNES	JW

Army Form C. 2118.

WAR DIARY
or
INTELLIGENCE SUMMARY.

(Erase heading not required.)

70 Bde RFA Nov 1918

Place	Date	Hour	Summary of Events and Information	Remarks and references to Appendices
ESNES	Nov 16			
	17		Brigade resting and refitting.	
	18			
	19			
	20			
	21			
	22			
	23			
	24			
	25			
	26			
	27		Inspected by G.O.C. 17th Division.	
	28		Resting & refitting.	
	29			
	30			

1/12/18

Smellie Capt RFA
for Lieut Col RFA
Cmdg 70 Bde RFA

War Diary

79th Bde. R.F.A.   November 1918

APPENDIX

I   Amm. Expended   A 8000   AX 2000
    (approx)   BX 3000

II Casualties   Killed   Officers NIL   O.R.   3
                 Wounded   "   NIL   "   30
                 Gassed   "   NIL   "   NIL

III Wastage (sickness)   Officers 2   O.R. 50

IV Horse Casualties Killed   4
                      Died   2
                      To M.V.S.   27
                      Destroyed   2

                              [signature] Capt R.F.A.
                              for Lieut Col. R.F.A.
                              Cmdg 79th Bde. R.F.A.

1/12/18

Army Form C. 2118.

WAR DIARY
INTELLIGENCE SUMMARY

December 1918

70th Bde. R.F.A.

Vol 41

Place	Date	Hour	Summary of Events and Information	Remarks and references to Appendices
ESNES	1			
	2			
	3		Resting and re-fitting. A number of minor despatches to U.K.	
	4			
	5			
	6			
MANANCOURT	7		Brigade marched to MANANCOURT en route for AIRAINES.	
MEAULTE	8		March continued, staying over for night — MEAULTE	
PONT NOYELLES	9		March resumed. Brigade arrived at PONT NOYELLES at 1 p.m.	
AIRAINES	10		AIRAINES reached at 5 p.m.	
	11			
	12			
	13		Resting and re-fitting. Training carried out. Sports. Education, etc.	
	14			
	15			
	16			
	17			
	18			
	19			

WAR DIARY

INTELLIGENCE SUMMARY 79th Bde. R.F.A.

December 1918

Army Form C. 2118.

Place	Date	Hour	Summary of Events and Information	Remarks and references to Appendices
AIRAINES	Dec 16		Refitting & training. Considerable time devoted to the sports and amusements of all ranks. Meeting covered stables, Recreation Rooms, etc.	
	20			
	21			
	22			
	23			
	24			
	25			
	26			
	27			
	28			
	29			
	30			
	31			

Swarren
Lieut Colonel R.F.A.
Commanding 79th Brigade R.F.A.

January 2nd 1919

WAR DIARY

Army Form C. 2118.

December 1918 — 79th Brigade R.F.A.

Summary of Events and Information

Casualties

Killed   Officers NIL   O.R. NIL
Wounded   do.   NIL   do. NIL
Wastage through sickness. do. 43

Animals

Killed   —
Wounded   —
L.M.V.S.   43
Destroyed   4
Died   3

Swanwick
Lieut-Colonel R.F.A.
Commanding 79th Brigade R.F.A.

January 2nd 1919

Army Form C. 2118.

WAR DIARY
or
INTELLIGENCE SUMMARY. 79th Bde. R.F.A.
(Erase heading not required.)

Vol 4. 2

Place	Date	Hour	Summary of Events and Information	Remarks and references to Appendices
AIRAINES	Jan 1-31		Rest & demobilising	

Inverarin
Lt. Col. R.F.A.
Cmdg. 79th Bde. R.F.A.

3/2/19.

Army Form C. 2118.

WAR DIARY
~~INTELLIGENCE SUMMARY~~ APPENDIX
(Erase heading not required.)

79th Bde. R.F.A.

Instructions regarding War Diaries and Intelligence Summaries are contained in F. S. Regs., Part II. and the Staff Manual respectively. Title pages will be prepared in manuscript.

Place	Date	Hour	Summary of Events and Information	Remarks and references to Appendices
AIRAINES	JAN 1919		Casualties	
				Officers O.R+
			Killed NIL NIL	
			Wounded NIL NIL	
			Wastage through Sickness NIL 16	
			Demobilised NIL 73	
			ANIMALS.	
			Killed NIL	
			Wounded NIL	
			To M.V.S. 33 horses 3 mules	
			Destroyed 1 mule	
			Died 1 horse	
			Demobilised 36 horses.	
	February 3rd 1919		J.W. Warren Lt. Col. R.F.A. Comdg. 79th Bde. R.F.A.	

Army Form C. 2118.

WAR DIARY
INTELLIGENCE SUMMARY.

(Erase heading not required.)

79th Brigade R.F.A.

February 1919   Vol 43

Place	Date	Hour	Summary of Events and Information	Remarks and references to Appendices
TRAINES	Feb. 1-28		Demobilizing	w/S.

Suwanen
Lieut Colonel R.F.A.
Commanding 79th Bde. R.F.A.

March 3rd 1919

Army Form C. 2118.

WAR DIARY
or
INTELLIGENCE SUMMARY.
(Erase heading not required.)

APPENDIX 79th. Bde. R.F.A.

Place	Date	Hour	Summary of Events and Information	Remarks and references to Appendices
ATTAINES	Feb 1919		Casualties. Officers ORs Killed NIL NIL Wounded NIL NIL Wastage through sickness 1 7 Demobilized 2 96 ANIMALS. Horses Mules Killed NIL NIL Wounded NIL NIL To M.V.S. 25 16 Destroyed 1 1 Died NIL NIL Demobilized 91 75 March 3rd 1919 Wiseman Lieut. Colonel R.F.A. Cdg. 79th. Bde. R.F.A.	

Army Form C. 2118.

WAR DIARY
~~INTELLIGENCE SUMMARY~~ 79th Bde. R.F.A.

(Erase heading not required.)

MARCH 1919.

M 44

Instructions regarding War Diaries and Intelligence Summaries are contained in F.S. Regs., Part II. and the Staff Manual respectively. Title pages will be prepared in manuscript.

Place	Date	Hour	Summary of Events and Information	Remarks and references to Appendices
Avesnes	1919 March 1st to 31st		Demobilizing.	

[signature] Cpt. R.A.
for O.C. 79th Bde. R.F.A.
Cmdg. 79th Bde. R.F.A.

April 5th 1919.

Army Form C. 2118.

WAR DIARY
or
~~INTELLIGENCE SUMMARY.~~ APPENDIX
79th Bde. R.F.A.

Place	Date	Hour	Summary of Events and Information	Remarks and references to Appendices
Divisions	1919 March 1–31		**Casualties**	
			Officers O.R.	
			Killed NIL NIL	
			Wounded NIL NIL	
			Missing through Sickness NIL 14	
			Demobilized Capt. A.L. Impey 85	
			Lieut. R.V. Gregory	
			Rev. Capt. G.J. Gallagher	
			Major K.K. Bell. DSO.	
			ANIMALS	
			Horses Mules	
			Killed NIL NIL	
			Wounded NIL NIL	
			To M.V.S. 1 NIL	
			Destroyed NIL NIL	
			Died NIL NIL	
			Demobilized 174 53	

April 5th 1919

J. Smith Capt.
for A/Col. R.F.A.
Commanding 79th Bde. R.F.A.

www.ingramcontent.com/pod-product-compliance
Lightning Source LLC
Chambersburg PA
CBHW080905230426
43664CB00016B/2730